TEA with *Presidential Families*

by Beulah Munshower Sommer and Pearl Dexter

Edited by R. Elizabeth Doucet

Printed in the U.S.A.

Book design by Olde English Tea Company, Inc.

Includes bibliographical references.

ISBN 0-9676682-0-4

Dedication: TGBTG

Frontispiece: *The First Ladies' Tea Party* by Pawinee McEntire

Inside Front Cover: *Tea for a Lady* by Pawinee McEntire

Back Cover: *Winter White House* by Pawinee McEntire

This first edition is limited to 5000 copies of which
this is No. 2091.

Published and distributed by Olde English Tea Company, Inc.
3 Devotion Road ~ P.O. Box 348-P, Scotland, CT 06264
Telephone: 1.888.456.8651
Web Site: www.teamag.com

Preface

For the past ten years my interest in tea has grown. I have been collecting books on tea, learning about all the different types, visiting tea rooms and hotels, and enjoying afternoon tea around the world. I have become so engaged in this pursuit that I have been on several "tea tours," learning more every day. In the course of my travels I was fortunate to meet Pearl Dexter, editor and publisher of *TEA A MAGAZINE*. Our mutual love of tea made us almost instant friends and she has, of course, taught me a great deal.

The next thing I knew, I was giving lectures on tea, titled "The History and Social Customs of Tea." What fun it has been, talking to fellow tea lovers in Delaware, the District of Columbia, Maryland, New York, Ohio, Pennsylvania, Texas, Virginia, North Carolina, and West Virginia.

All of this interest in tea and history led right back to Pearl Dexter. She suggested that I write an article for her magazine, which I did. The first was entitled "Celebrating Tea with White House China." Pearl said "How about expanding this idea of the article about tea and the White House?"

After some initial conversations and meetings we agreed to turn this idea into a book. I am not sure we realized at first the task we had assigned ourselves. It started with a bibliography offered to me by Miss Betty Monkman, Curator at the White House. I commenced research in many libraries, the foremost of which was Hood College in Frederick, Maryland. They seemed able to come up with any book I wanted and the list grew longer. Hundreds of letters were written; hundreds of telephone calls were made; thousands of miles were travelled; hundreds of people helped with anecdotes, photographs, and conversations; dozens of pictures were taken, and one more book always seemed to become essential reading. It seemed that almost daily one more source of help and information appeared.

The result is this first book on the subject of presidential families and the social, cultural, and historical significance of tea in their lives.

Beulah Munshower Sommer

Introduction

I am grateful for the enthusiastic and diligent work of my co-author Beulah Munshower Sommer.

* * * * *

The history of tea goes back thousands of years. Next to water, it is the most widely consumed beverage in the world. Its evolution as a drink has been both pleasurable and medicinal. Socially, it has graced the tables of royalty and commoners alike throughout the world.

When we need to be comforted or refreshed, we have a cup of tea. When important decisions need to be made, we often make them over a cup of tea.

Many kings and queens, princes and princesses, emperors and empresses, and other heads of state visit Washington. Invariably, through the years, they have been invited to the White House for tea. When heads of state from another country present a gift to our president, what do they give? A tea set! We encountered this over and over again in our reading and research. For example, HRH Prince Olav and HRH Martha of Norway gave Franklin and Eleanor Roosevelt a gift of a stunning Art Deco tea set. The Emperor of China gave Woodrow Wilson and Edith Bolling Galt a lovely Rose Medallion tea set as a wedding present. The Khruschevs gave the Kennedys a fabulous cloisonné tea service. A Japanese delegation presented a valuable tea set to President Buchanan's niece, who was his official hostess.

Taking tea has also been a social custom for the children of our presidents throughout the years. The young Kennedys had tea on the White House lawn, and President and Mrs. Hayes' little girl Fannie had a dainty tea set, as did the Monroes' daughters. President and Mrs. Benjamin Harrison's grandchildren enjoyed tea parties in the White House.

Tea played an important role with the founding families of this country. They passed on the tradition as well as the accoutrements that beautified their tea tables. You are cordially invited to travel through American history with all our presidential families as they take tea.

Pearl Dexter

ACKNOWLEDGMENTS

To everyone listed here, the authors express their thanks for your help in making this book possible.

Lori and Chip Amos, Dianne Atkins, Brock Arsenault, Frank Aucell, Kathryn Donaldson Baker, Laura Belman, Detra Bennett, Jean Buchholtz, Mrs. George Bush, Kelly Cobble, Jane and Richard Davenport, Bert Edwards, Connie Ewy, Sandy Fisher, Kathy Fliger, Anne and John Foltz, Mary Fry, Ingrid Gillilland, Sylvia Grossberg, Laura Hamilton, Pamela Harden, John Harney, Jeanette Harper, Mrs. Webb Hayes III, Eve Hill, James Hill, Donna and Hubert Hoover, William Jenney, Jana Jopson, Stephanie Kenyon, Lee Langston-Harrison, Margraret Larsen, Donna and Ron Lasko, Jobina Linkkila, King Laughlin, Judith McAlister, Betsy and Harry McAlpine, Debi McColgan, Barbara McMillan, Claire Murphy, Emily Murray, Willie Nocon, Valerie Peacock, Karen Peters, Ruth Ravitz, Ethel Schwengel, Thelma Seline, Margaret Shannon, Wade Slinde, Mrs. Robert Taft II, Mrs. William H. Taft III, James Wagner, Linda Wheland, and Natalie Whitney.

A special thank you to Wendy Lopes for introducing us to Pawinee McEntire, the artist to whom we are indebted for the cover of this book, and to R. Elizabeth Doucet, James Churchill Streeter Jr, and Jeff Burnham for their talent and dedication to this project.

Many people from the list below without exception have been helpful, enthusiastic, and very gracious. They may be archivists, communications officers, curators, directors, historians, interpretive rangers, librarians, museum aides, museum technicians, site managers, or have a variety of other titles. To all of them the authors are grateful for their invaluable assistance with this book.

Adams National Historic Site
President Chester A. Arthur State Historic Site
Ashlawn-Highland
The James Buchanan Foundation for the Preservation of Wheatland
George Bush Presidential Library and Museum
The Carter Presidential Center
Jimmy Carter Library
Chicago Historical Society
Grover Cleveland Birthplace
President Calvin Coolidge State Historic Site
Dumbarton House
Dwight D. Eisenhower Library/Museum
Eisenhower National Historic Site
Mamie Doud Eisenhower Birthplace Foundation, Inc.
Millard Fillmore Birthplace (Aurora Historical Society)
The Gerald R. Ford Presidential Museum/Library
Galena State Historic Sites
James A. Garfield National Historic Site
Greensboro Historical Museum
President Harding's Home
Harding Home and Memorial, Ohio Historical Society
Harlan House
President Benjamin Harrison Home
Grouseland, Home of William Henry Harrison
Rutherford B. Hayes Presidential Center
Hood College Beneficial - Hodson Library
Herbert Hoover Presidential Library/Museum
The Hermitage, The Home of Andrew Jackson
Illinois State Historical Library
Thomas Jefferson's Monticello
President Andrew Johnson Museum and Library
Lyndon Baines Johnson Library
John F. Kennedy Library and Museum
Ladies' Home Journal
Abraham Lincoln Museum
Lincoln Home National Historic Site
Mary Todd Lincoln Home
Robert Todd Lincoln's Hildene

Longfellow National Historic Site
First Ladies' Library, Home of Ida Saxton McKinley
McKinley Museum
The James Madison Museum
Marion County Historical Society
Middleton Place
Minnesota Historical Society
James Monroe Museum and Memorial Library
Montpelier
Mount Vernon Ladies' Association
National Society of the Colonial Dames of America
National Trust for Historic Preservation
The New York Historical Society
Richard Nixon Library and Birthplace
National Archives at College Park, Nixon Papers
The Pierce Brigade
The Pierce Homestead
The Pierce Manse
James K. Polk Memorial Association
Ronald Reagan Library
Franklin D. Roosevelt Library
Little White House State Historic Site, Franklin D. Roosevelt
Theodore Roosevelt Birthplace
Theodore Roosevelt Collection, The Houghton Library, Harvard
Sagamore Hill National Historic Site, Theodore Roosevelt's Home
The Smithsonian, American Museum of American History
William Howard Taft National Historic Site
Harry S Truman National Historic Site
Sherwood Forest Plantation, Home of President John Tyler
United States Department of the Interior
Martin Van Buren National Historic Site
Vermont Division of Historic Preservation
George Washington's Mount Vernon Estate & Gardens
The Western Reserve Historical Society
The White House Curator's Office
The White House Historical Society
The White House Volunteer Office
Woodrow Wilson Birthplace & Museum
Woodrow Wilson House Museum

TEA with *Presidential Families*

Contents

Left: Chinese tea chest that belonged to George and Martha Washington. 14x14x8 wood, covered with paper decorated with Chinese scenes, flowers, and hummingbirds; lid fastened with brass hinges.
Photograph courtesy of Smithsonian Institution.

Below: China Export teacup and saucer that belonged to George Washington.
Photograph by Pearl Dexter, taken with permission at the James Monroe Museum and Memorial Library, Fredericksburg, Virginia.

We may not have slept in any of the places where George did, but we had the good fortune to hold one of his teacups and saucers. George and Martha were both confirmed tea drinkers well before he became President of the United States in 1789.

Tea had become the preferred breakfast drink throughout British North America by the mid-eighteenth century. Tea was often shipped from the Orient in porcelain jars and chests lined with lead, some of which were highly decorative. It was relatively expensive and often transferred to locked tea caddies. At Mount Vernon, George Washington's breakfast included three cups of tea, without cream, with three small hoe cakes (Indian cornmeal) swimming in butter and honey.

In December of 1757 George sent to England for his first recorded order of tea: six pounds of best Hyson tea and six pounds of best green tea. Earlier that year he had ordered six teapots to be shipped to Mount Vernon. Orders and invoices listed a variety of teas that the Washingtons purchased, including Bohea, Congo, Green, Gunpowder, Hyson, Imperial, and Young Hyson. Household ledgers from their Philadelphia home and the farm at Mount Vernon listed practical and decorative accoutrements purchased specifically for tea: tea boards, tea caddies, tea

Right: Oval wooden tea tray that belonged to George and Martha Washington. 24 x 32 rosewood tray with inlaid floral design surrounded by a wreath of rosebuds intertwined; scalloped maple rim; and bronze handles.
Photograph courtesy of Smithsonian Institution.

chests, tea china, teacups, a pewter tea equipage, a copper tea kettle with chafing dish, teapots, tea sets, silver teaspoons, tea tables, and a silver-plated tea urn. Washington's slaves also had tea wares. One visitor described the furnishings of a slave home at Mount Vernon as having "A very poor chimney, a little kitchen furniture amid this misery—a tea-kettle and cups...."

Martha's granddaughter Nelly Custis Lewis (raised by George and Martha) recalled that "Later in the day, tea was served at sunset in summer and at candlelight in winter." General Lafayette was one of the many distinguished guests entertained by George and Martha. An 1860 engraving by Thomas Oldham Barlow depicts George Washington and Lafayette standing on the porch of Mount Vernon with Martha about to pour the tea.

Tea led the way in founding America. Because the Americans did not accede to England's Tea Act of 1773, tea was refused at many ports along the eastern seaboard: Edenton, Philadelphia, New York, Charleston, Greenwich, Annapolis, and Boston, where it was dumped into the harbor. In a letter to George William Fairfax, dated June 10, 1774, George Washington wrote: "in short the ministry may rely on it that Americans will never be tax'd without their own consent that the cause of Boston the despotick Measures in respect to it I mean now and is and ever will be considered as the cause of America (not that we approve their conduct in destroying the tea)."

Later during the Revolutionary War he gave specific instructions regarding tea in orders dated September 22, 1779: "...the tea is not included in the foregoing instruction, but is to be distributed as follows, reserving fifty pounds of the best quality for future disposal: one pound of the best kind to each General Officer, half a pound of the same to each field officer and head of a staff department and a quarter of a pound per man of the remainder to any other officer of the army who shall apply."

Although many Americans renounced tea as a social beverage during the Revolutionary War, it regained popularity when the war ended.

Friends and acquaintances often gave gifts of tea to the Washingtons. In the spring of 1784, a young guest asked his mother to send Martha Washington a little present of "something exquisite, the best quality of tea, for instance...."

New Jersey poet Philip Freneau wrote an ode to commemorate the departure of the *Empress of China*, the first American ship to trade directly with Canton:

> . . . *She now her eager course explores*
> *And soon shall greet Chinesian shores.*
> *From thence their fragrant TEAS to bring*
> *Without the leave of Britain's king;*
> *And PORCELAIN WARE, enchas'd in gold,*
> *The product of that finer mould.* . . .

Above: Cincinnati teapot 1784-1785
Photograph courtesy of
The Mount Vernon Ladies' Association.

The Chinese porcelain teapot known as the Cincinnati teapot was part of Washington's most famous set of china brought to America on the *Empress of China*. It is decorated with blue "Fitzhugh" borders and the arms of the Society of the Cincinnati in enamel colors. This china was intended for members of the Society of the Cincinnati, an hereditary order of French and American allied officers who had served in the Revolutionary War. Martha Washington willed the Cincinnati service to her grandson, George Washington Parke Custis. It is believed to be the only teapot among the 130 pieces remaining from the complete service.

While visiting at Mount Vernon in January of 1785, house guest Elkanah Watson recorded in his memoirs: "I was extremely oppressed with a severe cold and excessive coughing… As usual after retiring my coughing increased. When some time had elapsed, the door of my room was gently opened; and on drawing my bedcurtains, to my utter astonishment, I beheld Washington himself, standing at my bed-side with a bowl of hot tea in his hand. I was mortified, and distressed beyond expression. This little incident, occurring in common life with an ordinary man, would not have been noticed; but as a trait of the benevolence and private virtue of Washington, it deserved to be recorded."

The government moved to Philadelphia in December, 1790, where the President and his First Lady often entertained.

Artist Benjamin Henry Latrobe, along with other diarists, recorded taking tea at Mount Vernon. He also drew a sketch of taking tea on the porch in 1796. That same year the East India Company presented a monogrammed tea service to the Washingtons, each piece featuring Mrs. Washington's initials at the center as well as the names of all 15 states in the union at that time.

John Adams
Abigail Smith

Treasured by many Colonial American families, tea was an important way of socializing. While John Adams was serving in the Continental Congress, he engaged his statesman friend Elbridge Gerry, who was going home (to Massachusetts) on leave, to carry a canister of precious tea for Abigail to cheer her. Later he learned that the absent-minded Mr. Gerry gave the tea to his sister Mrs. Samuel Adams, John's cousin. Abigail had visited Mrs. Adams to ease her loneliness and was pleasantly surprised when the servant brought a tray of tea. Little did she know that it was her very own tea that she was drinking. John Adams purchased another canister of tea (a luxury at the time), and sent it home to Abigail by another carrier.

Abigail's closest friend, Mercy Otis, married John's friend James Warren. They visited each other often to discuss life, country, and philosophy over a warming dish of tea. But soon tea, "that baneful weed," as Abigail called it, tore them from a peaceable social life.

John Adams' diary mentioned tea many times. In 1771, he wrote of dining with friends and "spent the whole afternoon and drank green tea from Holland I hope, but don't know." Taxed tea from England was not a popular choice, thus leading up to the "Boston Tea Party" incident. On December 17, 1773, the pages in his diary read: "Last Night 3 Cargoes of Bohea Tea were emptied into the Sea. This Morning a Man of War sails. This is the most magnificent Movement of all. There is a Dignity, a Majesty, a Sublimity, in this last Effort of the Patriots, that I greatly admire. The People should never rise, without doing something to be remembered— something notable And striking. This Destruction of the Tea is so bold, so daring, so firm, intrepid and inflexible, and it must have so important Consequences, and so lasting, that I cant but consider it as an Epocha in History."

Tea was recognized as a healthy cure-all. Another entry in John's diary, dated June 21, 1779: "This Morning I found Mr. Marbois recovered of his Sea Sickness. I fell into Conversation with him,

Above: Eighteenth-century Chinese Export porcelain tea bowl and saucer, belonging to President and Mrs. John Adams.

Opposite Page: Eighteenth- century Chinese Export porcelain teacup, saucer, and teapot, decorated with a drooped-winged eagle, sunburst in sepia and gilt, monogrammed with "JA" on the eagle's shield of each piece, belonging to John Adams.

Photographs by Pearl Dexter—courtesy of the Adams National Historic Site in Quincy, Massachusetts.

about his illness, advised a Dish of Tea, which he readily accepted, told him he must learn to drink Tea in America in order to please the Ladies, who all drank Tea. That the american Ladies shone at the Tea Table. He said, he had heard they were very amiable and of agreeable Conversation."

John and Abigail Adams were the first occupants of the Presidential Mansion (the big white house on Pennsylvania Avenue in Washington, D.C.), today known to everyone as *The White House*—home of the President of the United States of America. When they moved in on November 16, 1800, the walls were not plastered, and the stairs not yet installed. To Abigail's dismay, most of her blue and white tea china was broken or missing when it finally arrived from Philadelphia. Many ladies called on Mrs. Adams and sent special invitations, including Mrs. George Washington. She spent much of her time returning over a dozen calls a day. The ladies were eager for an invitation from Abigail to the Presidential Mansion. Finally on New Year's Day in 1801, the President and his First Lady formally opened the mansion for a public housewarming party.

Chinese Export porcelain was quite popular. The blue and white tea set that had been broken was not easy to replace. The Adams National Historic Site exhibits a large drum-shaped tea pot and tea set, decorated with a drooped-winged eagle, sunburst in sepia and gilt, monogrammed with "JA" on the eagle's shield of each piece. It was undoubtedly made for John Adams, probably while he served as President. Herbal infusions became popular during and after the Revolutionary War—*The White House Cookbook* by Janet Erwin includes Abigail's recipe for Rose Petal Tea.

Third President   Thomas Jefferson   **1801-1809**

hostess Martha Wayles Skelton

So great was his passion for tea that Mr. Jefferson designed a specific polygonal-shaped Tea Room at his beloved Monticello to adjoin his parlor. Many guests left records of their experiences at Monticello, recounting how tea was served as a continuation of dinner. The men and women separated after the evening meal; later they rejoined to have tea, followed by fruit (and perhaps pastries).

The Tea Room houses a remarkable collection of portraits and plaster busts of personages vital in the history of the United States: George Washington, Benjamin Franklin, John Paul Jones, and the Marquis de Lafayette. Also on exhibit are bronze busts of the Roman emperors Tiberius, Nero, Otho, and Vespasian, as well as sixteen engraved miniature portraits.

Eighteenth-century teas were ranked for their quality in descending order as Hyson, Souchong, Congou, and Bohea. Thomas Jefferson, the third president of the United States, regularly purchased tea all his adult life, approximately twenty pounds per year. Although his first recorded order was for Bohea, Jefferson's taste later changed to Hyson, which became his favorite from 1809-1816.

Two hundred years later Lady Bird Johnson remarked that *many things happen over a cup of tea.* Jefferson presaged this comment by entertaining his many friends and foreign visitors at tea. In his Tea Room, upon the small lap desk he had designed, he wrote and edited the draft of the Declaration of Independence in 1776.

Jefferson's wife Martha died in 1782, leaving him a widower for nineteen years before he ascended to the presidency. As president, he elected to include his monogram along with a fleur-de-lis design in blue and gold on French china. Dolley Madison occasionally presided over social affairs, and later his daughter Martha ("Patsy") acted as his hostess at the White House for many years. She and her husband, Thomas Mann Randolph, Jr., and their family resided at Monticello with Thomas Jefferson until he died in 1826.

Facing Page: The tearoom at Monticello
Watercolor by Kathy Fliger.

12

James Madison
Dolley Payne Todd

Over a cup of tea one day, Martha Washington talked enthusiastically to widowed Dolley Payne Todd about her friend James Madison. At this tea the seed was planted for their future union (which took place in September of 1794), when Mrs. Washington went so far as to suggest a marriage between her two friends.

James and Dolley Madison may have been influenced by Thomas Jefferson, while James was Secretary of State in Jefferson's Presidency, by designating the room in their Montpelier home that adjoined her bedchamber as a "tea room."

Invitations to the Madisons' were very much sought after because of the kind and vivacious hostess Dolley. Occasionally President Jefferson called on Dolley to preside at his social

Above: Silver service set, early nineteenth century, belonging to President James Madison.
©Collection of The New-York Historical Society.

functions in the White House. In 1809 James Madison became President and Dolley blossomed even more as Washington's first hostess. For more than eight years she was a highly successful official hostess, giving teas and receptions to important visitors. She delighted in having smaller, intimate gatherings, at which her congeniality and charm sans cérémonie were a great attraction to her guests.

Right: Invitation from Mr. & Mrs. Madison to Mr. & Mrs. Nourse.
Courtesy of Dumbarton House, Washington, D.C.

Tea was customarily served at breakfast, sometimes in the afternoon, and particularly after the evening meal. Dolley was fond of using her beautiful silver tea service on these occasions and she was reknown for her desserts: layer cake, seed cake, and ice cream. It is presumed that invitations were sometimes sent just for evening tea: "Mr. and Mrs. Madison request the pleasure of Mrs. and Mrs. Nourse's company to tea on Tuesday Evening next."

John Jacob Astor, a friend of the Madisons, made part of his fortune in the tea trade. He may have made a gift to them of the tea he brought back from China.

James Monroe
Elizabeth Kortright

Above: Cup and saucer, belonging to James Monroe.

James Monroe was educated at the College of William and Mary in Williamsburg, Virginia, and he studied law under Thomas Jefferson. In 1786, at the age of 27, Monroe married beautiful Elizabeth Kortwright of New York and moved with her to Fredericksburg, Virginia.

Four years later, he became a United States Senator and in 1794 was appointed by President George Washington as Minister to France during the Reign of Terror. James and Elizabeth lived in France for three years, where Elizabeth courageously aided in the release of Lafayette's wife.

Returning home, he became Governor of Virginia in 1799 and moved his family to Highland (later named Ashlawn by subsequent owners, but now referred to by both names) in Albemarle County, Virginia, where their first guests were James and Dolley Madison.

It is interesting to note that Monroe, Madison, Jefferson, and Washington were all friends. In 1799 when Washington lived at Mt. Vernon, Jefferson was Vice President, Madison was soon to become Secretary of State, and Monroe was Governor of Virginia. One can easily imagine the four of them with their wives taking tea together.

Just as Elizabeth would have learned about the taking of tea at an early age, she carried on the tradition for their daughters Eliza and Maria with children's china tea sets. Depending upon the number of children and dolls attending the tea parties, where they would emulate the elegant manners of their mother, they often mixed and matched the different sets. These tea sets came from China, and were likely to have been exported to England where they were handpainted, possibly at the Lowestoft porcelain

Below: Children's tea set belonging to the children of Elizabeth and James Monroe.

Photographs by Pearl Dexter—Courtesy of the James Monroe Museum and Memorial Library.

Above: French tea table with marble top, tea caddy, and teacup and saucer, belonging to James Monroe.

Right: Early nineteenth-century tea caddy, belonging to James Monroe.

Photographs by Pearl Dexter—Courtesy of the James Monroe Museum and Memorial Library.

factory in Suffolk. Maria eventually gave them to her children and they were passed down a few more generations before being donated to the James Monroe Museum in the 1920s or 1930s by Rose de Chine Gouverneur, Maria's granddaughter.

The lifestyle of James and Elizabeth Monroe was undoubtedly influenced by their sojourns in Europe, having lived in society circles in France and England. While living in Europe, the Monroes purchased a Louis XVI desk, a handsome tea table and tea caddy, and other furnishings and objêts d'art. Elizabeth Monroe introduced some aspects of

French culture when she was First Lady in the White House, one of which was to alter social and official customs to resemble those of formal European courts. Attended by servants in livery, she entertained one evening a week at receptions, dressed in black velvet and pearls. On another evening each week, James and Elizabeth kept open house, at which they served iced cakes, coffee, and tea.

John Quincy Adams
Louisa Catherine Johnson

Although Abigail Adams preferred Chinese Export, Louisa and John Quincy Adams seemed to prefer German china, as his diary noted. In his *Letters on Silesia,* John Quincy Adams mentioned that he and Mrs. Adams visited Meissen, which he spoke of as the great manufacturing center of Saxon porcelain. On February 18, 1810, John Quincy Adams recorded in his financial ledger that he had purchased a large quantity of Meissen. This china was also used by his grandson, Brooks Adams.

While Minister to the Netherlands and Prussia, John and Louisa travelled extensively throughout Europe. Louisa Catherine Johnson was born in London in 1775 (the only First Lady to have been born outside the United States). Her father served as United States Counsul after 1790; her mother was English. She and John Quincy Adams first met in Nantes, France, where the Johnsons were living, when Louisa was four and he was twelve, travelling through France with his father. Later, when his father was President of the United States, they met again in London. By then Louisa had become a beautiful young lady with delicate features and strawberry blond hair— John was Minister to the Netherlands at the time. They married in London in 1797.

Family history attributes the acquisition of the porcelain teapot with the silver spout to Louisa Catherine Adams. It was purchased secondhand, probably in Dresden, and got broken in their travels; Louisa had it repaired in the Netherlands. The teapot is an inverted pear-shape with a rosebud finial and branch handle. The spout has a silver cover with incised decoration on top of a clown's head. There are raised fluted rays from the top end at the curve of the body of the teapot, and the lower area is enclosed with rococo feathers, forming a cartouche for four overglaze initials in floral

Above and right: Portraits of John Quincy Adams and Louisa Adams.
Courtesy of the Adams National Historic Site in Quincy, Massachusetts.

Opposite Page: Sèvres porcelain tea caddy and teacup and saucer, with pencilled profile bust of Chysppe and Chillon.
Photographs by Pearl Dexter, courtesy of the Adams National Historic Site in Quincy, Massachusetts.

forms: JCMV. Being purchased secondhand, the initials therefore have no relevance to the Adams family. It bears the mark of King's Porcelain Manufactory (KPM), Berlin.

Above and right: German porcelain teapot, c.1770-1775, belonging to Louisa Catherine Adams.
Courtesy of the Adams National Historic Site in Quincy, Massachusetts.

The Adams National Historic Site in Quincy, Massachusetts, is rich with tea accoutrements. Louisa's English silver tea set is on display, along with a Sèvres porcelain tea set decorated with miniature portraits of classical personages Aesop, Chillon, Democrites, Aristotle, Anacharsis, Pittacus, and Chrysppe.

When John Quincy Adams became President in 1824 he and Mrs. Adams regularly held levees every other Wednesday evening from about eight to ten p.m. Guests were treated to tea, coffee, cakes, jellies, ice cream, wines, cordials, and liquors.

Louisa was always an elegant hostess at official entertainments and receptions. Although her husband lost his bid for reelection she was still the gracious hostess for the last official reception.

Andrew Jackson
Rachel Donelson Robards
hostess Emily Donelson

In 1791, Andrew Jackson married the kindly, unpretentious Rachel Robards. A country girl, Rachel found the city of Washington's bustling society to be daunting. She received countless invitations, including many to take tea. In an inventory of their household belongings it was noted that they owned a white and gilt French china tea service of 156 pieces.

They had no children but delighted in Rachel's ten brothers and sisters and their children. Sadly, Rachel died four months before her husband became President. Emily, a favorite niece of Rachel's, had married her cousin, Andrew Jackson Donelson. He had been reared by Rachel and Andrew and later was to be President Jackson's private secretary.

Emily had often acted as hostess of the White House and attended many parties and teas. When the role of White House hostess was thrust upon her, due to Rachel's death, she was well prepared. Emily capably and enthusiastically assumed her new social duties.

Below: Sterling silver tea infuser–American made by Webster Company.
Courtesy of The Hermitage: Home of President Andrew Jackson, Nashville, TN

On the President's silver tea service, along with the maker's mark, "LV&Co," his name, "Andrew Jackson," is engraved on the inner rim of the base of each piece. In the invoice of June 4, 1833, President Jackson purchased a number of silver tea accoutrements from L. Veron and Company.

The teapot was $38.18
1 Sugar Dish $30.13
1 Cream Pot $16.07
1 Slop bowl $21.10
On that same invoice appears another item:
1 Splendid Tea Urn with Heater $215.90

From humble origins, Jackson had ascended to the highest office in the land.

Above: Silver tea service made by L. Veron & Co., purchased by Andrew Jackson in 1833.
Courtesy of The Hermitage: Home of President Andrew Jackson, Nashville, TN

Martin Van Buren
Hannah Hoes
hostess Angelica Singleton

Tea was imported into Holland in the early seventeenth century and the Dutch took up the custom long before the British. In Van Buren's era, spice and honey cakes, seafood and game pastries, olykecks, and china tea constituted high afternoon tea. A lump of sugar was placed between the teeth as the drinker sucked the hot tea. Dutch New Yorkers flavored their tea with various herbs, including costly saffron.

Martin Van Buren and Hannah Hoes, both of Dutch descent, had known each other from early childhood. They had four sons. When they lived in Albany, contemporary letters indicate that Hannah entertained often. She was described as having a "loving, gentle disposition." In 1819 she died of tuberculosis.

When Van Buren became President he had been a widower eighteen years. He had not remarried and moved into the White House with his four bachelor sons. Dolley Madison was living nearby, still reigning as matriarch of Washington society. Having helped George Washington find a bride, she decided to promote a match between her young relative Angelica Singleton and one of Van Buren's sons. Dolley arranged for a visit to the White House for her niece and thus a meeting between Angelica and Abraham, the President's eldest son. The outcome was as Dolley had hoped and a wedding soon took place. From that time on Angelica acted as the White House hostess.

When the President's son John went to England in 1841 he wrote back to his father: "I have bought you a China teapot... ...The teapot and candlesticks go down in the Rockland today to your address, care of Butler & Vosburgh, Stuyvesant Landing."

After President Van Buren left office and moved to his home along the Hudson River, he enjoyed using his elegant china tea tervice. An excerpt from his writings in 1845 decries the loss of some china. Writing to a friend, James K. Paulding, he said, "There is not a house in the country where there has been so much destruction of china and glass as in mine. If those articles are as good manure as muslin curtains, my farm cannot fail to flourish, for I have scarcely a field which has not been covered with them through the ashery, the great storehouse for broken articles... ...the female waiter... had broken the principal part of a very beautiful tea and breakfast set which I valued above everything in the House. So much so that I have actually sent to Paris to have former trespasses repaired by additions of the same articles which I have never been able to find anywhere except in the President's House."

Right: Unmarked gold-banded porcelain teapot (with missing lid) and sugar bowl with lid, c.1835-45.
Courtesy of National Park Service, Martin Van Buren National Historic Site, Kinderhook, NY

William Harrison was descended from England's King Henry II (1207-1272), from his paternal grandmother's family. His father, Benjamin Harrison V (1726-1791), was a signer of the Declaration of Independence. In 1795 he married Anna Symnes and they had ten children. Their grandson Benjamin Harrison became the twenty-third President of the United States.

The military and politics were full- time careers for William Harrison. His run for the presidency was considered the first modern presidential campaign. Not wearing a hat, gloves, or overcoat during his one hour and forty minute inaugural address on a cold March afternoon and later getting caught in the rain on his way to the White House contributed to

President Harrison's early demise. His wife was too ill ever to come to Washington; their widowed daughter-in-law Jane Irwin Harrison acted as hostess for only a month before William Harrison died, just thirty-one days after his inauguration.

His wife Anna lived for a number of years after her husband's death in their splendid home, Grouseland, in Vincennes, Indiana. A cobalt blue, white, and gold Spode china tea set is now displayed on the tea table in the parlor at Grouseland. In the upstairs bedroom a pink, blue, and white Liverpool tea set, probably used by Anna and her daughters, is on a tea table.

Above: Anna Harrison
From the painting of *The First Ladies*
by Pawinee McIntire

When John and Letitia Tyler moved into the White House, she had suffered a stroke a few years before. Their daughter-in-law, Priscilla Cooper Tyler, wife of their son Robert, very willingly served as his hostess at official events. Southern hospitality prevailed and teas and receptions were numerous.

Mrs. Letitia Tyler died in 1842. She and John Tyler had had eight children, one of whom, Letitia Tyler Semple, briefly served as White House hostess. Young Letitia described the simpler side of Washington life: "We breakfasted at eight-thirty and dined at three o'clock, except on state occasions, of course, and had tea served after our daily drive, to escape from all the environments of political and social cares and duties, because my father's time was rarely his own. . . ." In 1844 he took a second wife, Julia Gardiner, a stunning young socialite from New York. This union produced seven more children. Although busy with her ever-growing family, Julia presided over glamorous teas, receptions, and parties during the remainder of his presidency.

During the time Tyler was President, China opened its ports to world trade as a result of the Opium Wars with England. This was an important event in the tea trade, making it more plentiful and less expensive. Charles Dickens and Daniel Webster were guests at the White House during his administration. One of the punches served was "Daniel Webster Punch," which contained rum, brandy, champagne, arrack menschino, lemon juice, sugar, and strong green tea.

When Tyler's Presidency ended, he and Julia retired to his home, Sherwood Forest Plantation in Charles City, Virginia, where Julia often served tea in the drawing room. In 1845, Julia became ill but recovered fully. She gave credit for her recovery to black tea, and she reported to her mother, "I find that black tea is better for me than *coffee* which I thought I never could live without. I have acquired a fondness for black tea and scarcely regret the coffee."

John Tyler died in 1862 at the Exchange Hotel in Richmond, Virginia. Years later when she was visiting her son Lyon Gardiner Tyler, president of the College of William and Mary, Julia suffered a stroke while staying at the same hotel. Offered a strong drink by doctors consulting on her illness, she quietly shook her head and said "tea." *Tea* was the last word she uttered before dying.

Spode china and a Sheffield silver tea urn remain in the family collection at Sherwood Forest Plantation..

Facing page: John Tyler and Julia Tyler.
Courtesy of Mrs. Tyler Stuart and Sherwood Forest Plantation, Charles City, VA.

Right: Silver urn and Spode china tea set.
Courtesy of Sherwood Forest Plantation, Charles City, VA.

James Polk
Sarah Childress

The era of Polk's administration was one of courtly grace and sentiment, characterized by sedate, candlelit tea parties with musicians playing soft music in the background. Mrs. Polk did not condone the gay teas and receptions given by her predecessor, and frivolity, including dancing, was frowned upon. Although she did appear at her husband's Inaugural Ball, she declined to dance.

James K. Polk and Sarah Childress Polk were both southern born, he in North Carolina, she in Tennessee, where Polk moved at age ten with his family. Sarah, the daughter of wealthy Captain Joel Childress and his wife Elizabeth, acquired an excellent higher education, unusual for a woman at that time. No doubt she participated in afternoon teas. They apparently met through a mutual friend, Andrew Jackson. James, who had studied classics and later law, was a member of the Tennessee legislature when he and Sarah married in 1824.

Her education stood Sarah in good stead in Washington, both socially and intellectually. They joined the most select social circles during the administrations of Van Buren, Jackson, and John Quincy Adams, and she assisted her husband with his speeches and correspondence. Tea was often served to the Polks' relatives upstairs in Sarah's private apartments. She served tea to General Edmund P. Gaines when he flattered her with a New Year's Day visit, wearing his Tennessee sword.

During the years the Polks occupied the White House, interest mounted in growing tea in the United States—a Dr. Julius Smith successfully cultivated tea plants in Greenville, South Carolina.

Above: Sarah Polk and James Polk.

Below: German porcelain teacup and saucer used by the Polks at the White House.

Photographs courtesy of James K. Polk Ancestral Home, Columbia, TN.

Zachary Taylor
Margaret Mackall Smith

Mrs. Zachary Taylor (Peggy) is said to have vowed to her husband, that, if he returned safely from the Mexican War, she would never again go into society. That vow was kept, and she relegated her entertaining to her sitting room, for friends and family. Their daughter Mary Elizabeth Bliss beautifully fulfilled all official social fuctions.

Mary presided at delightful weekly tea parties on the lawn, where the Marine Band's rousing marches induced her father to mingle with the guests. An approachable, "folksy" man, he shook hands with many as he passed. When the tea parties were held indoors, elegantly attired waiters circulated with trays of cakes and tarts of all descriptions.

Although Mrs. Taylor seldom attended official functions, a set of White House china was commissioned by British potters. The Staffordshire blue pattern features a blue and white American eagle with an ornate border design.

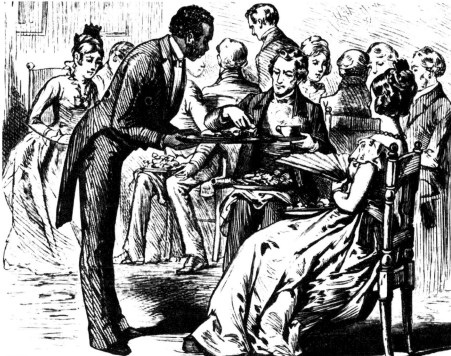

Above: Tea party in Washington in Taylor's time.

Photograph courtesy of CORBIS-BETTMANN.

29

Millard Fillmore and his wife Abigail Powers bonded because of their mutual interest in schooling. They both encouraged the creation of the first permanent White House library, located in the Oval Room; Abigail spent many happy hours selecting and arranging books.

Due to an injured ankle Abigail passed many of the social duties of the White House on to her daughter Mary Abigail, who entertained her mother by playing the piano and harp in the Oval Room.

Mary Abigail would have hosted the White House teas and receptions. Abigail Powers Fillmore owned a lovely pink luster teapot which she gave to her cousin Sophia Powers Pangburn. It was cherished and used by three generations of Pangburns and is now the property of the Millard Fillmore Museum.

During Fillmore's presidency, American clipper ships were swiftly sailing the seas. The *Sea Witch* (designed for the New York–China Tea Trade) had cut over sixty days from the normal travel time between New York and San Francisco.

While England's East Indiamen waited, American clippers sailed off with cargoes of tea at double the ordinary weight.

Above and left: The *Sea Witch*.

Drawings by Edward A. Wilson from *Clipper Ship Days* by John Jennings.

Franklin Pierce
Jane Means Appleton

Above: Tea set at the The Pierce
Homestead, Hillsborough, NH.

Below: Teacup and saucer at the The
Pierce Homestead, Hillsborough, NH.

Photographs courtesy of Donna Hoover.

In 1820, Franklin Pierce entered Bowdoin College in Maine, where his future father-in-law had served as president. Nathaniel Hawthorne began his studies there the following year, and the two became lifelong friends. In Hawthorne's class was another man of letters, Henry Wadsworth Longfellow. After Bowdoin, Pierce studied law and was admitted to the bar in 1827.

His marriage to the devout and retiring Jane Means Appleton took place in 1834 in Amherst, New Hampshire. They were to lose all of their children, and the frail Mrs. Pierce never recovered. She opposed her husband's bid for the presidency and due to poor health, rarely carried out public social duties. These were left to her aunt by marriage Abby Kent Means and friend Varina Davis. Jane Pierce presided only at an occasional small tea party in the White House.

The shield was a popular motif, showing up on the dinnerware of Franklin Pierce in a simple pattern richly decorated with cobalt blue on a gold pointelle border and rim of 23k gold, made by Haviland and Company in France. The entire dinner service with accoutrements cost $536.24, a sizeable sum in the 1850s.

Buchanan lost the true love of his life and never married—his niece Harriet Lane acted as his hostess. He had had a distinguished career, including tours of duty in Russia and England, before becoming President. Miss Lane accompanied her uncle to London and was the official hostess at the London Embassy.

After the tragic Pierce administration, Washington welcomed the lively entertaining of President Buchanan and his niece Harriet Lane. They entertained the Prince of Wales, later Edward VII, in 1860, using the dinnerware purchased by Franklin Pierce. During his term of office, there is no record of a bill for a dining service; therefore it is presumed that the service purchased by President Pierce was used. Both President Buchanan and his niece, Harriet Lane, owned a large service of china. The President's personal china was a handsome pink-banded Sèvres set, decorated with flowers, and Harriet's china, purchased in France, had a red edge.

During the Presidency of James Buchanan a hothouse and garden (known as The Botanical Gardens) were established in Washington, D.C., to experiment with imported tea plants. Interested individuals could attempt cultivation in their own areas by applying for some of the plants. They were distributed in 1860—one consignment per congressional district.

In May 1860 a large delegation of Japanese dignitaries came to the United States. The President and Miss Lane greeted them with gracious formality. They left many gifts at the White House, including an exquisite tea set inlaid with pearls and gold. At the time it was valued at $3,000.00 Unfortunately, its whereabouts are now unknown, but this drawing shows the Japanese presenting a large box to their host. Perhaps the tea service was enclosed!

Below: May 17, 1860. The Japanese ambassadors being received at the White House by President James Buchanan.

Photograph courtesy of BALDWIN H. WARD/ CORBIS-BETTMANN.

Abraham Lincoln
Mary Todd

Above: Gorham silver tea and coffee service presented to Mrs. Abraham Lincoln when she was First Lady.
Photograph by Rick Vargas, courtesy of Smithsonian Institution.

Below: Porcelain tea set (unmarked); gift from Lincoln and colleagues.
Photograph courtesy of Lincoln College, Lincoln, Illinois.

When Abraham and Mary Todd Lincoln settled in Springfield, Illinois, they often had friends and visitors join them for tea. Purchases of tea and coffee are recorded at two Springfield stores. A clerk at one of them recalled Mr. Lincoln's often saying, "Colonel, my wife tells me we are out of tea. Put up a pound of the best."

A complete Gorham silver tea service was presented to Mrs. Lincoln when she was First Lady. The Todd coat of arms and initials are on the tray.

Shortly after moving into the White House, Mary Todd Lincoln purchased a brilliant dinner set that of course included a full tea service. It features an American eagle breaking through clouds against a brilliant sun, with wings outstretched, holding a bundle of arrows in the left talon and an olive branch in the right one over the banner, "E Pluribus Unum." Mrs. Lincoln changed the original blue border to a purplish rose color called "solferino"—the fashion rage of the day, lavishly accented with gold tracery and bands. When Mrs. Lincoln entertained, her critics accused her of unpatriotic extravagance, yet after her son Willie's death in 1862, she curtailed her entertaining and they accused her of shirking her social duties.

Abraham Lincoln and several legal colleagues from the Eighth Judicial Circuit purchased a tea set as a wedding gift for a young woman from Clinton, Illinois. He carried it in his saddlebag and presented it to her at her home. This twelve-piece set included an unusual tray.

33

Andrew Johnson
Eliza McCardle

Andrew Johnson married Eliza McCardle when he was eighteen and she only sixteen. He started his political career as Alderman of Greeneville, Tennessee in 1828, later to become Mayor, Member of the House of Representatives, State Senator, U.S. Representative, Governor of Tennessee, U.S. Senator, Military Governor of Tennessee, Vice President, and President of the U.S. He was stunned by the news of Abraham Lincoln's assassination and used an office in the Treasury Building as a temporary White House, thus giving Mrs. Lincoln all the time she needed to relocate.

When Johnson did move into the White House he brought his entire family with him, including grandchildren. Mrs. Johnson had developed slow consumption earlier in life and became an invalid. As First Lady she appeared publicly only twice, once in 1866 at a reception for Queen Emma of the Sandwich (Hawaiian) Islands and at a birthday party for her husband in 1867. Their daughter, Martha Patterson, acted as the President's official White House hostess. She had often been a guest at the Mansion during the Polks' administration. She was unpretentious, but gracious.

Before becoming President, in 1859 Johnson had been involved in the idea of a transcontinental railroad. Trains running through the desert could transport tea, silks, and other goods west. Johnson had always been interested in tea. Members of Congress were able to distribute tea seedlings in February and March, 1860, from the tea hothouse in Washington established during the presidency of James Buchanan. In 1860 his son Robert, a member of the Tennessee House of Representatives, wrote to him requesting that some tea plants be sent to Mrs. Brown and Mrs. Hubbard in Nashville.

Probably because of his interest in the railroad, he had been given an unusual novelty teapot in the shape of a locomotive, which he used every day for his tea. The boiler received the tea and brewed

The publisher of *Tea with Presidential Families* regrets the error on page 35 in the Andrew Johnson chapter. It was stated "In fact, President Andrew Johnson was the father-in-law of Davis, who had been the President of the Confederacy." He was NOT his father-in-law. Please accept our apologies.

Thank you.
Sincerely,

Pearl Dexter

Pearl Dexter

it, then discharged it through a spigot. A miniature steam-whistle and a little bell indicated when the beverage was ready. On the brass tender were sugar, glasses, and a container for cognac. The sides carried racks for cigars and a tiny music box played eight popular tunes. On the side was a Latin inscription that said in English, "God helps those who help themselves." Also on the side in gold was "President Jefferson Davis"—the teapot had at one time belonged to him. In fact, President Andrew Johnson was the father-in-law of Davis, who had been the President of the Confederacy. The locomotive was used daily and when a new envoy would present his credentials, he would be served tea from this incredible locomotive teapot.

It was during Johnson's administration that the Great Tea Race took place, leaving China for London on May 28, 1866. The first two ships to arrive at London's docks were the *Ariel* and the *Taeping*, carrying over two million pounds of tea.

Ulysses S. Grant
Julia Dent

Ulysses Grant was born into modest surroundings. His father sought a West Point appointment for Ulysses, who was reluctant to go. However, an appointment was secured—he graduated as a second lieutenant and was assigned to Jefferson Barracks, near St. Louis. He soon met and fell in love with Julia Dent. They maintained a happy lifelong marriage through failures and successes. President Lincoln admired General Grant and invited him and Mrs. Grant to accompany the Lincolns to Ford's Theater the night he was assassinated. Fortunately, circumstances prevented them from accepting the invitation.

After serving as Secretary of War, Grant was elected President in 1868.

Julia was happy to live in the White House and gave lavish parties. American artist William E. Seaton created a range of original

floral decorations that the Grant White House had France's Haviland and Company's painter-engraver transfer to the center of each plate. While living in the White House a number of her family often visited. Julia's father Colonel Dent attended most White House receptions and it has been said that he liked to drink his tea from fine china.

It wasn't until the Grants' trip abroad, following his presidency, that Ulysses Grant drank tea with the Viceroy of China and the Emperor of Japan.

In her memoirs, Julia wrote, "When I had finished my cup of delicious tea, Lady Li took my hand and led me to the drawing room..." She goes on, "We visited a teahouse; that is, a house where they prepare tea for export. It was very interesting to watch the pretty little Japanese girls picking and assorting tea."

In her memoirs she talks about her lovely tea set of Sheffield plate.

Facing page: Original Haviland china from The Grant White House.
Courtesy of Galena State Historic Sites, U. S. Grant's Home.

Rutherford B. Hayes
Lucy Ware Webb

When Rutherford Birchard Hayes was born in Delaware, Ohio, his father had died two and a half months earlier. An uncle helped finance his education when he attended private schools in Ohio and Connecticut. He graduated from Kenyan College in Ohio and then entered Harvard Law School. When he returned to Cincinnati, he became not only a successful lawyer but also a bridegroom. His bride was Lucy Ware Webb, a graduate of Wesleyan Female College. Together they had a large family—one daughter and seven sons.

During the Civil War Hayes became an army general and was nominated for Congress while still in the army. President Lincoln was assassinated, President Johnson's impeachment trial took place, and Ulysses S. Grant was elected President before Hayes was named the Republican candidate for President.

Mrs. Hayes always felt that the White House was her personal home and, according to her beliefs, served no liquor. She did offer lemonade, coffee, and tea at many parties and receptions. Lucy Hayes established a pleasant routine in her everyday life which included an early afternoon lunch consisting of bread and butter, cold meats, and tea. When she held Saturday receptions during the holidays, she often asked her young house guests to stand in various rooms to encourage conversation.

In 1880 President and Mrs. Hayes entertained at a superlative reception for the diplomatic corps. The newspaper report was quick to point out that lemonade and coffee were served at supper and tea in the hall upstairs.

Mrs. Hayes was able to juggle home and official entertaining with seeming ease and grace. She influenced the design of the

Above: Teapot belonging to Lucy Hayes.

Photograph by Pearl Dexter, courtesy of the James Monroe Law Office Museum and Memorial Library, Fredericksburg, Virginia.

Above: Teacup and saucer from the Hayes set in the shape of an inverted mandarin's hat. .

Photograph by John Foltz, courtesy of Rutherford B. Hayes Presidential Center, Spiegel Grove, Fremont, Ohio.

Below: USA's tea "dollar"—The face of the medal bears the head of Washington. The reverse side, in raised letters, has the substance of the lease. The medal is larger than a U.S. silver dollar and is 1¾" in diameter.

Courtesy Museum Collections, Minnesota Historical Society.

562-piece porcelain service for the Executive Mansion by suggesting the use of the flora and fauna of the United States as decoration on the new china. This remarkable set of china was recognized for its American look, with only one exception, the teacup—an unusual piece resembling an inverted mandarin's hat. The cup and saucer were both decorated with a rendition of a tea plant. The handle was the stem of a tea plant and the inside of the cup painted a delicate green.

When Rutherford Hayes was inaugurated, one of his appointments was William LeDuc of Minnesota as Commissioner of Agriculture. While travelling in the South, the commissioner noticed that many of the tea plants distributed by the Patent Office were growing luxuriantly. He was so impressed that he applied for an appropriation to carry on further experiments in tea culture. LeDuc later took samples of American-grown tea to Mr. Low, of A. A. Low Bros. Co., a leading New York firm in tea, with a fleet of sixteen clipper ships. One of them was the *Houqua*, famous for fast runs from China to the United States. He was encouraged by his meetings and sought to find the best locality in the South to carry out tea experiments. He met Henry A. Middleton, the owner of Middleton Plantation, near Charleston, South Carolina, where in 1800 Michaux, the French botanist, had planted the first tea plant in America. Middleton gave the government a twenty-year lease on two hundred acres for LeDuc's U.S. Experimental Tea Farm—the cost: one dollar!

"One silver dollar. No greenback," said Mr. Middleton. The next day the commissioner returned with the lease and the silver dollar. Upon his return to Washington he decided that a special medal should be made for Middleton. Three were struck at the Philadelphia mint: one was presented to Middleton, another given to President Hayes, and LeDuc kept the third.

James Abram Garfield
Lucretia Rudolph

James Abram Garfield was the last President to be born in a log cabin, in 1831. He became a college administrator, married Lucretia "Crete" Rudolph in 1858, was admitted to the Ohio bar in 1860, achieved the rank of major general in the Civil War, and later became State Senator and a U. S. Representative before he was elected President of the United States in 1880.

Lucretia Garfield, although shunning publicity, graciously took up her duties as First Lady. Tea was included at White House social gatherings and it is known that the President was very partial to tea. Two of his favorite recipes for blending tea were published in *The Presidents' Cookbook*.

Above: Embroidered velvet tea cozy used during the presidential campaign of 1880.

SPICE TEA

Water	Mint leaves
Sugar	Orange juice
Black tea	Lemon juice
Allspice	

Boil together 1 cup water and 1 cup sugar for 5 minutes. Then add 2 teaspoons black tea, ½ teaspoon allspice, and 2 fresh mint leaves (dried will do, if fresh mint is not available). Cover the pan and allow the mixture to steep at least 10 minutes. Strain and add to the liquid 2 quarts boiling water, ¾ cup orange juice and 6 to 8 tablespoons lemon juice. Bring the mixture to a boil and serve. Serves 12.

Below: Copper tea kettle.

Photographs by John Foltz, courtesy of The Western Reserve Historical Society, James A. Garfield National Historic Site, "Lawnfield," Mentor, Ohio.

The President's wife skillfully embroidered an unusual tea cozy, possibly for her husband. The worn but still lovely cozy is embellished with naturalistic white flowers and sheaves of grain embroidered to give a chenille-like effect.

The cozy and a copper tea kettle that belonged to the Garfields are at the restored Garfield home, which is a national historic site in Mentor, Ohio.

President Garfield was assassinated in 1881 by one of his supporters, Charles Guiteau, who had come to the White House seeking a diplomatic post but was politely turned down. The disgruntled man was mentally unstable and viewed his act as being politically necessary. The President was attended by well-meaning physicians, but he succumbed to blood poisoning two and a half months later, induced no doubt by their unsanitary examinations. Vice President Chester Arthur succeeded him as President of the United States.

Garfield's plucky widow took a very active role in preserving her husband's memory. She had a vault for his personal letters, papers, and books set up in the Garfield homestead.

Chester Arthur
Ellen Lewis Herndon
Hostess Mary Arthur McElroy

Chester Arthur's wife, Ellen Lewis Herndon, died before he became President of the United States. His sister Mary Arthur McElroy was his hostess during the White House years.

Chester Arthur, born in Fairfield, Vermont, did not stay attached to his Vermont roots, unlike President Calvin Coolidge. His father, William Arthur, was born in Ireland and became a Baptist minister in the United States. Not much is known about Chester Arthur's early life, as his father was transferred from one parish to another. Young Chester moved seven times in his childhood, living in Vermont and New York State. In 1845 he entered Union College in Schenectady, New York. An excellent student, he was elected to Phi Beta Kappa and after graduation studied law. He became the principal of North Pownal Academy in Vermont, where three years after he left, James Garfield was hired as a teacher.

While practicing law he married Ellen Lewis Herndon, daughter of an aristocratic Virginia family. Her family connections and gracious manners were invaluable influences in Chester Arthur's life. Unfortunately, she died at age forty-two, before Arthur became Vice President under President Garfield—Garfield's assassination thrust Arthur into the White House.

In 1881, the Executive Mansion purchased from J. W. Boteler and Son:
1 Dozen Dresden Tea Cups and Saucers
1 Dozen Haviland Tea Cups and Saucers

President Arthur was a cultured man who loved to socialize—he preferred afternoon teas and large receptions as a means of entertaining. During his administration the White House was redecorated, and he asked his sister Mary Arthur McElroy to be his hostess. She relished her work at the White House and initiated the custom of serving tea to hundreds of guests at public receptions. Her brother, the President, always impeccably dressed, was at his best at these social functions.

Right: Tea on the White House lawn.

Drawing by Pamela Harden

Grover Cleveland had held positions as teacher, editor, lawyer, Mayor of Buffalo, New York, and governor of New York before being elected President. A larger-than-life figure, his personality was a contradiction between jovial and carefree and stern and duty-bound.

President and Mrs. Cleveland were married in the White House, the first presidential couple to do so. Up until that time the bachelor President had not done much entertaining. Mrs. Cleveland changed all that and immediately became a social success. They began to give receptions and dinners, with great formality.

However, one of Mrs. Cleveland's innovations was to give informal teas in the Green Room. They were often held on Saturdays so that women from non-political circles could attend—this immediately endeared her to many people. Mrs. Cleveland bought 191 teacups and 190 saucers, and in 1895 she bought 400 plates and 200 teacups and saucers with pink roses and green leaves—a Theodore breakfast set made by Haviland, Limoges.

An amusing incident occurred at a tea at when she was entertaining a group of foreign students. The students, unaccustomed to the ritual of afternoon tea, decided to do everything Mrs. Cleveland did so they would make no mistakes. When the First Lady poured a little milk into her saucer, so did they. It was only when she placed it on the floor for her kitten that they realized something was amiss.

Mrs. Cleveland loved living in the White House and entertaining. When they left, she promised to return, which they did after her husband's re-election four years later.

Above: Frances Folsom Cleveland
From the painting of *The First Ladies*
by Pawinee McIntire

Benjamin Harrison
Caroline Lavinia Scott

Benjamin Harrison was born at his grand-father William Henry Harrison's (the ninth United States president) home in 1833 in North Bend, Ohio. Having had unlimited access to his grandfather's private library, Benjamin acquired a deep interest in history and politics. He married the talented Caroline Lavinia Scott ("Carrie") in 1853 at her home in Oxford, Ohio. Carrie was a graduate of the Oxford Female Institute and an accomplished pianist and artist. She took an ardent interest in the painting of china, which she had taught in Indianapolis. Her beautiful work was displayed on teapots and a myriad of other items, which she often gave to her friends. Benjamin was United States Senator from Indiana just before he was elected President in 1888.

When the Harrisons moved into the White House, their grown son and daughter and their families took up residence with them, creating a lively atmosphere. The young grandchildren enjoyed tea and cookies in the White House nursery with their mothers. Mary Lord Scott Dimmick, Mrs. Harrison's niece, also came to live with them when she became a young widow.

Opposite page and below: Porcelain teapot hand-painted by Caroline Harrison.

Below right: Caroline Harrison's art tools.

Opposite page: Mrs. James Robert McKee (seated on the left), President Harrison's daughter, and his daughter-in-law, Mrs. Russell B. Harrison (seated on the right) enjoying tea and cookies in the White House nursery with President Benjamin Harrison's grandchildren: (Marthena Harrison (reaching into the bowl), Mary McKee (nibbling a cookie), and Benjamin ("Baby") McKee (in the rocker).

Photographs courtesy of the President Benjamin Harrison Home, Indianapolis, IN.

Mrs. Harrison was also a tireless hostess. Their charming daughter Mary McKee helped her mother with the busy social schedule, often standing by her side at receptions and teas.

Deciding to hold china painting classes in the White House, Caroline enlisted the aid of her former teacher, Paul Putzki. As a decorative artist, she designed a distinctive new set of White House china, adorned with goldenrod and cornstalks, symbols of American beauty and bounty. Small tea plates were included in the new set. Caroline Harrison also established the White House China Collection.

She died while her husband was still in office and her daughter Mary McKee became her father's official hostess.

Benjamin Harrison later married his wife's widowed niece, Mary Dimmick, and they had a daughter, Elizabeth.

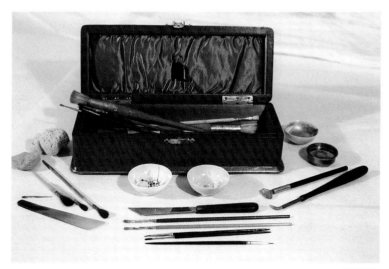

How India Tea Was Advertised in 1897

Before William McKinley became President, he was a distinguished Civil War soldier, lawyer, member of Congress, and Governor of Ohio. He married a wealthy young woman whose childhood home in Canton, Ohio is now the First Ladies' Library.

McKinley became President in 1897. At that time the tea industry recognized the merits of advertising and used a painting of Queen Victoria and President McKinley in an advertisement for the back cover of the October, 1897 *Ladies' Home Journal*. Also, in the same year the U.S. Tea Importation Act was passed. This law required the government to set tea standards and discourage shipments of tea of questionable quality. It remained in effect until 1997.

Left: Back cover page advertisement which appeared in the *Ladies' Home Journal* for October, 1897.
Print copied from *All About Tea* by William H. Ukers, first published in 1935 by Tea and Coffee Trade Journal and reprinted by Hyperion Press in 1996.

48

Despite her many illnesses, Mrs. McKinley enjoyed the social life of the capital. She was, however, never far from her devoted husband and was able to officiate at some functions, although the Vice-President's wife, Mrs. Garret Hobart, was usually the acting hostess. When friends called on Mrs. McKinley, she would welcome them warmly and ask if they would like a cup of tea.

Like most women of her time, she possessed some lovely tea ware.

Top Right: Cup and saucer, Oriental ware, medallion design; it belonged to Mrs. Ida Saxton McKinley.

Below Right: Teapot and lid, bamboo covered handle, blue on white with pink and white daisy flower pattern; used in the McKinley home in Canton, Ohio.

Photographs courtesy of the McKinley Museum and National Memorial/Stark County Historical Society, Canton, Ohio.

49

Theodore Roosevelt was born in the city of New York into a family of wealth and status. He graduated from Harvard and studied at Columbia Law School. His young wife died soon after the birth of their daughter Alice, and his mother died the same day. Two years later he married Edith Kermit Carow, an acquaintance since childhood. Edith successfully raised a large family, including her step-daughter, Alice.

Moving rapidly through political ranks, Theodore became Governor of New York and then Vice President. He drank his tea from an oversized tea cup every afternoon. When President McKinley was assassinated Roosevelt became our twenty-sixth president.

The Roosevelt children were a happy group and at times became somewhat obstreperous. On one occasion Quentin, leading a group of his friends, proved himself to be a disruptive force when his mother was having tea with an Italian diplomat and an army officer. The diplomat was wearing a monocle and Quentin was intrigued by it. He and his cohorts mimicked the diplomat by using watch crystals as monocles. They climbed up to a skylight to have a better look at the proceedings taking place below. His mother realized what he was doing and called out his name. The startled diplomat looked up, following Edith's gaze. His eyes widened and the monocle plopped into his tea.

Above: Edith Roosevelt on a picnic in Falls Church, 1907.
Photograph courtesy of Theodore Rooosevelt Collection, Harvard College Library.

Alice and Nicholas Longworth's wedding was a social highlight of the Roosevelt administration. Alice was very fond of drinking Jackson's of Piccadilly Earl Grey tea, a blend she had drunk from childhood. A popular Washington hostess, she continued to serve Earl Grey in tall glasses with silver holders, or sometimes in Rose Medallion cups.

President Roosevelt liked adding lemon and mint leaves to his sweetened black tea. Mrs. Roosevelt frequently entertained at the teas which were held weekly during the social season. Ladies wrote to her and requested an invitation, and lists were composed for Mrs. Roosevelt's approval. The number invited varied from a few hundred to as many as six hundred. Mrs. Roosevelt received her guests with the help of Cabinet wives and various family members. To avoid shaking so many hands, she carried a bouquet of orchids.

She made the White House the social center of Washington and the public waited in eager anticipation to read the newspaper accounts of the Roosevelt family.

Right: Dining room at the Roosevelt family's home on West 57th Street, New York, NY.

William Howard Taft was born into a prominent family in Cincinnati, Ohio. He graduated from Yale and returned home to practice law. There he met and married Helen Herron, the daughter of a lawyer whose law partner had been President Hayes. As a young girl she had been entertained at the White House and had a great desire to be the hostess there herself.

As Taft's career advanced, Helen was thrilled with the good positions he gained that she felt sure would put him on the road to the presidency. She delighted in her role as wife of the Governor General of the Philippines, where she entertained in great style.

Theodore Roosevelt and William Taft became good friends and after serving as Secretary of War, Roosevelt offered his friend two jobs—Chief Justice of the Supreme Court or a chance to become President of the United States. Helen urged him to try for the presidency. Taft acquiesced and with Roosevelt's help became our 27th President.

Mrs. Taft was very happy to be the hostess at the White House. On inauguration day she arranged a luncheon and later the same day a tea for her husband's Yale classmates. Her first Diplomatic Tea was held March 12th, at which all the Diplomatic Corps was received. Sometimes she held garden parties, where waiters served tea from tables set up under the trees.

One special social event during the Taft White House years was a coming-out tea for their daughter, attended by twelve hundred guests. Small afternoon teas were also hosted by Mrs. Taft where olive sandwiches, cakes, and tea for thirty guests would be the order of the day.

The President enjoyed social events in the White House and at his wife's invitation attended afternoon tea receptions for congressional wives. The most glamorous event was probably a party to commemorate the Tafts' silver wedding anniversary. A silver teapot was one of the gifts.

It was due to Mrs. Taft that thousands of cherry trees were planted in Washington. These bring seasonal delight to all who view them. After serving as President, William Howard Taft became Chief Justice of the Supreme Court, his life's ambition.

Above: Helen Taft

Woodrow Wilson and his first wife Ellen Louise Axson were both children of Presbyterian ministers. Woodrow Wilson attended Princeton, followed by law school at the University of Virginia. After a long courtship (they had known each other since childhood), they married at her grandparents' home in Savannah, Georgia, in 1885. He became President of Princeton, Governor of New Jersey, and then President of the United States in 1913. Ellen Axson supported her husband in every way. The closely-knit First Family, including their three daughters, Margaret, Eleanor, and Jessie, often enjoyed tea time together. Two large social functions in the White House were the marriages of two of the Wilsons' daughters. Ellen studied art briefly in New York, and when they moved into the White House a studio was set up for her there. Mrs. Wilson was a student of Robert Vonnoh, who painted a beautiful family portrait of her with the Wilson daughters during at their summer White House at Cornish, New Hampshire. Unfortunately, Mrs. Wilson died of Bright's disease one year later.

Facing Page: Portrait of Mrs. Woodrow Wilson and her three daughters, Margaret, Eleanor, and Jessie. Oil on canvas, dated 1913, by Robert William Vonnoh (1858-1933).
Courtesy of National Trust for Historic Preservation, Woodrow Wilson House Museum.

Woodrow Wilson's second wife was Edith Bolling Galt, a wealthy Washington widow. She met Woodrow Wilson over a cup of tea. Out walking with a cousin of the President, she was invited to tea afterward, but by happenstance they met the President in the hall. He had been playing golf with a Dr. Grayson. It was decided that the four of them would have tea together. Thus began a wonderful friendship which eventually led to marriage.

Mrs. Wilson's memoirs are full of references to tea, including one time when the President prepared tea on the south portico of the White House.. He proclaimed the fact that he had never prepared tea before and then demonstrated his lack of expertise by pouring nearly all the tea from the caddy into the teapot, so that the resulting beverage was virtually undrinkable, more like lye than tea..

It was during Wilson's administration that an official White House set of china was purchased for the first time from an American manufacturer, Lenox.

Facing Page, top: Tea tins on stove shelf in the kitchen of the Wilson home on "S" Street, Washington, D.C.
Photograph by Pearl Dexter, taken at the Woodrow Wilson House Museum.

In the afternoons, President and Mrs. Wilson received foreign ambassadors and their wives for an informal cup of tea and scheduled a group every half hour. Mrs. Wilson felt that this was a perfect way to get to know people and she enjoyed these occasions. The President and his wife always savored teatime on the *Mayflower*, the official presidential yacht. The graduating classes of schools in the Washington area were invited to the White House for tea. Any time a group of friends would get together, tea would be served.

There was, however, one time when an invitation to the White House for tea was declined. The Suffragettes were picketing the White House to demand votes for women. It was a very cold and windy day, so President Wilson asked the butler to invite the ladies into the White House to get warm and have a cup of hot tea. They refused his invitation!

Facing Page, center: Flow Blue plate and cup and saucer that belonged to Edith Wilson's grandmother.
Photograph by Pearl Dexter, taken at the Woodrow Wilson House Museum.

Facing Page, bottom: Teapot on the pantry shelves in the kitchen of the Wilson home on "S" Street, Washington, D.C. The kitchen and pantry are preserved to look as they did when President Wilson and his wife Edith Wilson lived there..
Photograph by Pearl Dexter, taken at the Woodrow Wilson House Museum.

Right: Chinese famille-rose medallion teapot from a tea set given by the Chinese ambassador to President and Mrs. Wilson in 1915, as a wedding gift.
Photograph by Lucinda Eddy, courtesy of Woodrow Wilson Birthplace.

Warren Gamaliel Harding was born and raised in Ohio. As a young man he learned to run a press while working for the weekly *Caledonia Argus*. When he was only nineteen he bought the *Marion Star* with two partners. Later he acquired full ownership, and when he married Florence Kling, five years his senior, in 1891, her managerial skills as circulation director helped to make the newspaper a financial success while her husband's political career thrived. Before entering the White House, Harding was State Senator of Ohio, Lieutenant Governor of Ohio, and U. S. Senator.

It is customary for the wife of the outgoing president to invite the wife of the incoming president for tea. After Warren Harding had been elected, Mrs. Wilson invited the new First Lady to tea. Some time later, Mrs. Harding invited the former First Lady, Mrs. Edith Wilson, back to the White House to share a private tea. They both took a special interest in the welfare of veterans.

Due to President Wilson's illness the mansion and grounds had been closed to the public. Mrs. Harding reopened them and energetically entertained, making sure to include veterans at many garden parties.

Above: Invitation from the Hardings
Courtesy of Marion County Historical Society.

Once a school group received an unexpected invitation for tea. Many years later one of the guests told of her special day in a letter to Mrs. Beulah Sommer..

"Many years ago the music teachers in Washington, DC selected the seventh graders of the Public Schools to form a choral group to sing to President and Mrs. Warren G. Harding at a ceremony at the Lincoln Memorial.

I wasn't chosen, but my best friend Lillian Rosenfeld was. She was a little timid about going to town alone so she asked me to go along for company. At the Memorial we parted company; she to go up to the platform at the top of the steps, I to stay below with the observers.

Before the singing could start, a tremendous wind and rain storm blew up. The gale of wind seemed to blow away all of the observers and many of the young choral group. I ran up the steps to be with my friend and saw a small group of children surrounding a dejected-looking President and his wife.

He soon brightened and said, "Here's what we shall do. Come with me to the White House. We can have tea and cookies there and you can sing to me and Mrs. Harding in the East Room."

We all walked arm in arm, chatting gleefully while trying not to step in the puddles the rain had left. When we arrived at the White House we became a bit subdued and awed by the huge East Room and its sparkling chandeliers.

After we sang several songs we each received a huge cookie with our tea. Then we filed out quietly as we shook hands with the gracious and smiling President and his wife.

But for them, what might have been a very disappointing finale turned out to be a lovely visit to the big White House on Pennsylvania Avenue."

Thelma Seline

Above: Nineteenth-century Yixing teapot.

Facing Page: Silver tea urn (front and back), made by Rogers & Bros., Waterbury, Connecticut, engraved with Kling family name.

Photographs by Al Tozer, courtesy of Marion County Historical Society.

Mrs. Harding had a nineteenth-century Yixing teapot that eventually was donated to the Marion County Historical Society in Marion, Ohio, along with her family's silver tea urn that had belonged to her father, Amos Kling.

Calvin Coolidge
Grace Anna Goodhue

Calvin Coolidge had graduated from Amherst College, was admitted to the bar in 1897, opened a law office in Northampton, Massachusetts, married Grace Goodhue in 1905, was Mayor of Northampton, State Senator, Lieutenant Governor, and Governor of Massachusetts. He was elected Vice President on Harding's ticket for president in 1920. Coolidge was awakened while on vacation at his father's farm in Plymouth Notch, Vermont, at 2:47 a.m. on August 3, 1923, to be informed of the death of President Harding. His father, who was a notary public, gave him the presidential oath.

Grace Coolidge had been a lip-reading instructor for the Clarke Institute for the Deaf in Northampton before she married Calvin. She later served as president on the board of trustees for the school. Her son John also served on the board. Grace's sensitivity was an asset for a White House hostess. When President Coolidge and Grace attended teas, it was agreed between them that they would excuse themselves at six o'clock. If she sometimes wanted to stay later, he would give her pleading looks.

For Christmas 1925 the President and Mrs. Coolidge received from a friend a beautiful sterling silver tea set made by T. Kirkpatrick & Company, New York.

When the Amherst Glee Club visited Washington, the President wittily entertained them for tea. Another favorite guest for tea was Alice Roosevelt Longworth with her daughter Pauline. After Grace had been hostess at a very crowded reception, Calvin said that if Mrs. Harding had garden parties, they could have sidewalk tea parties to accommodate the throngs.

Grace Coolidge had many social demands for her time—she was seen

Above: The Coolidge Homestead in Plymouth Notch, Vermont

Photographed by Pearl Dexter at The Vermont Division for Historic Preservation, President Calvin Coolidge State Historic Site.

Right: Sterling silver tea set made by
T. Kirkpatrick & Company, New York.

at concerts, balls, receptions, dinners, teas, and tea dances. Ever hospitable herself, Grace didn't turn a hair when all manner of callers came to her "At Homes," some sitting right at the tea table and helping themselves liberally to the refreshments. She was a brilliant hostess and the teas that she gave in the Red Room were enormously popular. These were usually small groups of twenty or thirty guests, people who had made requests to be so honored. It was the custom at that time to leave a note at the White House asking to be received—"leaving a card" was still considered proper. She also entertained at tea the wives of cabinet members.

The Coolidges did more entertaining at the White House than any previous administration. On one occasion Mrs. Coolidge noticed one of the guests putting her tea napkin into her handbag. Later the lady reached in for her handkerchief and realized what she had done. As she pulled the White House tea napkin from her handbag everyone could see that there were holes in it! No doubt the fun-loving Grace found this highly amusing. On another occasion, while entertaining a group of three hundred professional men at tea, a guest was observed putting a tea napkin in his pocket. This one, however, was not returned.

The Coolidges loved dogs; sometimes they came to tea by invitation, at other times they mysteriously appeared, probably urged on by the President, who loved to play jokes on Grace. Two of their most famous dogs were white collies, Rob Roy and Prudence Prim. Prudence Prim enjoyed teas, making the round of the guests, hoping for a treat.

Mrs. Coolidge was an expert needlewoman. She hoped to inspire future First Ladies to leave something personal at the White House. A copy of her experimental panel crocheted for the Lincoln bed coverlet at the White House, "A Coverlet for the Ages," is seen next to the Élite pattern Limoges tea cup that the Coolidges used in their private quarters of the White House, along with the nineteenth-century folding fan that Mrs. Coolidge had acquired on her visit to Havana in 1928.

Facing page-Clockwise: Nineteenth-century folding fan—Casa Calvet Prado 86, Habana.
Élite pattern of Limoges tea cup and saucer.
Experimental panel crocheted by Grace Coolidge for "A Coverlet for the Ages."

Photographed by Pearl Dexter at
The Vermont Division for Historic
Preservation, President Calvin
Coolidge State Historic Site.

Lou Hoover loved to entertain, and she made even a small affair into a large social tea or dinner, hosting many tea parties. Often two teas were in progress in the Green Room and the Red Room at the same time, and sometimes afternoon tea was held on the White House Lawn, depending upon the season. Lace cookies, a favorite dessert of hers, were often on the tea menu.

The King and Queen of Siam were the first monarchs to be entertained at the White House. A formal dinner was given and a tea the following day.

Mrs. Hoover's tea guests were from many different organizations, including the League of Women Voters and wives of federal officials and congressmen. An invitation to Mrs. Jesse DePriest, wife of Congressman Oscar DePriest from Chicago, brought both criticism and praise, because she was the first African-American woman to be invited to a White House Tea.

Lou Hoover's social secretary, Mrs. Edith G. Bowman, remarked on the affection the Hoovers demonstrated to each other while she and her brother were having tea with the First Lady one afternoon on the second floor of the White House.

When Mr. and Mrs. Hoover entertained Lord and Lady Astor at tea, the President, who seldom attended teas, arrived a little late, apologized for being tardy, and politely requested the Astors' permission to smoke a cigar after he drank the orangeade that had been served to him. He placed the cigar wrapper in his empty glass. The server refilled his glass, not realizing that it was not really empty—the cigar wrapper floated to the top. The President carefully fished it out and placed it in a nearby ashtray. It has been said that Mrs. Hoover used signals to direct servants at White House functions, such as touching her hair, or moving a glass.

Opposite page: Britannia teapot, c. 1888. Made in U.S. by Wm. Vogel. Bun-shaped body with decoratively embossed circular spread foot, applied scroll handle, hooked spout, tall neck, and slightly domed, stepped lid with wooden finial.

Below: Pewter teapot, late nineteenth century. Made in England, possibly by Shaw and Fisher. Spherical body with applied scroll handle, swan neck spout, and hinged lid with strawberry finial, raised on four paw feet with mask head terminals; ivory insulators; copper lined.

Photographs courtesy of Herbert Hoover Presidential Library/Museum.

Mrs. Hoover's fondness for tea led her to collect Britannia and pewter teapots. Although many of her porcelain tea accoutrements still reside with the Hoover family, some of Lou Hoover's collection of Britannia and pewter teapots were donated to the the Herbert Hoover Library by Margaret Hoover Brigham.

Hand-delivered invitations for tea were often sent to area high school students while the Hoovers were in the White House. An alumna of Georgetown Visitation Preparatory School remembers:

"I do not recall the exact date, but I can put it in the proper time frame. It was during the fall-winter months of my senior year in high school. While election of a new President occurred in November, Inauguration Day was held in March, and we were still wallowing in the effects of the Great Depression. What could be more exciting than a personal invitation, hand delivered from the White House?

The little white card invited me to tea at four p.m. with Mrs. Herbert Hoover. Similar invitations were delivered to my classmates and graduating classes of other high schools.

At the proper time we assembled at the East Entrance of the White House wearing our best bib and tucker and, of course, white kid gloves (we dressed in uniforms at school). Mrs. Hoover, so dignified and rather statuesque, greeted us warmly.

It was my first visit to the White House. We were led through the handsomely furnished historic rooms to the large dining room. A beautiful silver tea service graced the table and tea was served in dainty china cups together with an abundance of small cookies. Mrs. Hoover mingled and chatted with each of us individually. It was an elegant experience.

I think what amused [my friend] was my aftermath story. All the national banks were closed when President Rooosevelt took office. When they finally opened, I had the great sum of $5 and decided I would start a savings account. So I went to a small bank and was promptly asked who had recommended me. Nobody had. The only identification I possessed in my wallet was the little white invitation from the White House marked NON TRANSFERABLE. So the bank clerk opened my account and on the line that read "recommended by" wrote, *The White House*.

Thirty-second President Franklin Delano Roosevelt
Anna Eleanor Roosevelt

1933-1945

Above: Mrs. Franklin D. Roosevelt and former Premier of France Edouard Herriot having tea at the White House.
Photograph courtesy UPI/CORBIS-Bettmann.

President and Mrs. Roosevelt both grew up in households where tea was taken in the afternoon as a matter of course, alone or with her family, friends, and houseguests, so it is not surprising to know that they often entertained at tea while living in the White House. Former Premier of France, Edouard Herriot, was entertained by Mrs. Franklin D. Roosevelt when he was sent by his country as envoy to the Roosevelt economic conferences in 1933. She was very careful to attend to the needs of her houseguests, serving Winston Churchill terribly weak tea as requested. One of their first guests was Madame Chiang Kai-shek. Mrs. Roosevelt took great pains to serve some very special Chinese tea, supposedly a hundred years old. When she mentioned the great age of the tea to her guest, Madame Chiang Kai-shek replied, "In my country, tea kept so long is used only for medicinal purposes."

One of the highlights of the year 1935 for the National Society, Colonial Dames of America, was an invitation to tea in the White House from Mrs. Roosevelt, who was a member of the Society in the state of New York. Tea was served in the state dining-room and, following her usual custom at such times, the hostess mingled informally with the guests, making them welcome with her own unaffected kindness.

In 1936, the Elex Club of General Electric, during a trip to Washington, was extended an invitation to tea at the White House. It is described in great detail, climaxing in the reception room where they awaited the arrival of Mrs. Franklin Roosevelt. In a moment the huge doors opened and Mrs. Roosevelt said, "Good afternoon, everybody. I'm so glad you came to see me." She was dressed in a blue flowered print afternoon dress. They went into the dining room, where a long table was ready with tea and fancy cakes.

Above: Mrs. Eleanor Roosevelt with Lady Redding in Bristol, England, having tea made from the blitz-stove.
Photograph courtesy UPI/CORBIS-Bettmann.

Below: Art Deco tea set made by David Andersen, c. 1930s, given to President and Mrs. Roosevelt from HRH Prince Olav and HRH Princess Martha of Norway.
Photograph courtesy of White House Historical Association and the Franklin D Roosevelt Library, Hyde Park, New York.

President and Mrs. Roosevelt entertained HRH Prince Olav and HRH Princess Martha of Norway at Hyde Park with a tea and a picnic in 1939. The royal couple sent a stunning red enamel and gold Art Deco tea set to the Roosevelts as a remembrance of their visit.

Eleanor Roosevelt entertained at so many teas that she sometimes had two in a row. This kind of event made a lot of work for the staff as one group would be scheduled at four o'clock and another at five o'clock.

Sometimes she invited wives of Cabinet members to receive at teas with her. Eight teas a week was not unusual. In 1939, 9,211 people came to tea. On Inauguration Day, 1941, 4,000 guests were served. Sandwiches and cakes were consumed along with thirty gallons of tea.

From Mrs. Roosevelt's memoirs we learn of one tea to which no one came. Three hundred and seventy-five people had been scheduled, and all was in readiness. Investigation revealed that a person new in the office had misinterpreted checkmarks on the list and had not sent the invitations. Contrary to her staff's fears, Mrs. Roosevelt sent the food to institutions in the District and had an unexpected free hour.

President Roosevelt spent a considerable amount of time in Warm Springs, Georgia. A pantry cupboard there brims with teacups and teapots. Tea sets that were used there are on display, including one given to the President by his aunt Laura Delano, made by Copeland-Spode, and an English Ridgeway Old Ivory Bedford Ware tea set.

Below: Pantry cupboard at Little White House State Historic Site in Warm Springs, GA.
Photograph courtesy of Janet and Gerald Finnegan–The Creative Source.

Below: English sterling silver water kettle, with a black bone handle and finial with warmer stand; maker Ellis Silver Co., New York City, a branch of Ellis & Co., Birmingham, England. English silver teapot, maker Andrew Fogelberg, 1797—known to have been used by Anna Roosevelt, but uncertain whether or not the teapot may have belonged to Anna's mother Eleanor Roosevelt, or Anna's grandmother.

Photograph courtesy Franklin D. Roosevelt Library, Hyde Park, New York.

Curtis Roosevelt, grandson to the President, remembers his mother Anna's using a magnificent sterling silver tea set for her teas. Curtis, Eleanor Seagraves, and John Boettiger gave it to the Franklin D. Roosevelt Library in Hyde Park, New York, in 1978.

Harry S Truman
Elizabeth (Bess) Virginia Wallace

Harry S Truman married Bess Wallace, whom he had known since fifth grade, when they were both in their thirties. The former haberdasher had to face some of the most difficult decisions in United States history.

President and Mrs. Truman were very hospitable people. Contrary to media reports of Mrs. Truman's shyness and unwillingness to take part in the Washington social scene, nothing could be further from the truth. It is true that early in her tenure as First Lady, when she was entertaining lady journalists at tea, she did not give them much information about herself. She declared that she was only the President's wife and mother of his child.

However, a study of the records of the White House Social Office during the time of the Truman administration reveals a constant flow of visitors into the White House, where Mrs. Truman displayed much graciousness and charm. Teas averaged more than one a week. Some of those invited to tea were: Women's National Farm/Garden Association; District of Columbia Dental Assistants Society; National Conference of Christians and Jews; War Hospitality Committee; and White House Clerical Staff. Tea at these affairs was often poured by Mrs. Helm, who was social secretary to several First Ladies. It is said that she could pour a cup of tea, never spill a drop, and keep up a running conversation at the same time.

Mrs. Truman's social calendar listed sixteen teas in one month, and another month eight teas are noted for hospitalized veterans. Whenever possible, the President was present at these teas. He was not announced but just came quietly into the room. In addition to large teas for organizations, Mrs. Truman hosted small groups. At one tea she entertained Mrs. Roosevelt and Grandma Moses. Sometimes the President would join the tea guests and when asked to play the piano, he would do so. Imagine a lovely tea at the White House with the President of the United States supplying the musical accompaniment.

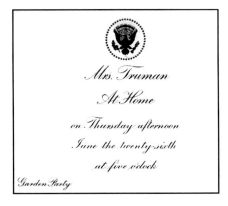

Above: Invitation from the Trumans

Courtesy of National Park Service, Harry S Truman National Historic Site.

Below: Mrs. Truman, President Truman, Grandma Moses, and Mrs. Eleanor Roosevelt.

Photograph by Jackie Martin. Courtesy of Harry S Truman Library, Independence, Missouri.

During the time the White House was being renovated in 1948-1952, the Trumans lived at Blair House. When they returned Mrs. Truman held a series of teas, giving government officials the opportunity to tour the refurbished mansion.

Mrs. Truman also attended teas held outside the White House. She went to the House and Embassy Tour Tea to benefit the Home for Incurables, and the Fashion Tea for the benefit of the Christ Child Farm for Convalescent Children.

When President Truman was in office, teas were given for every woman government employee in the Washington area. This is hard to believe in our time, but the government employee force was much smaller then.

Harry and Bess Truman were private people whose house changed very little after returning home to Independence from the White House. Their lifestyle reflected practicality and simplicity. Many tea accoutrements belonging to the Trumans are on display at the Harry S Truman National Historic Site in Independence, Missouri. The beautiful silver tea service, which includes a tea kettle, has Bess Truman's initials engraved on the teapot. The museum also houses the Trumans' Chinese Famille-rose export porcelain tea set with the rose medallion pattern, and a pair of simple dark green teapots.

Below left: Silver tea kettle and teapot; maker Platería Ortega, Mexico City, Mexico.
Below right: Chinese Famille-rose export porcelain teapot and a pair of teacups and saucers.

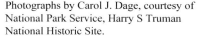

Photographs by Carol J. Dage, courtesy of National Park Service, Harry S Truman National Historic Site.

Dwight D. Eisenhower
Mamie Geneva Doud

From all reports, President and Mrs. Dwight Eisenhower were tea lovers. Their tea guests included notables such as Madame Chiang Kai-shek, Mrs. Anthony Eden, and groups such as Red Cross nurses, 450 Wives of Representatives and 1,500 Republican women!

Sometimes President and Mrs. Eisenhower entertained together. This was the case upon the occasion of the visit of Mrs. Chiang Kai-shek, who was personally invited to tea by the President in 1953.

Dear Madame Chiang,

". . . .Mrs. Eisenhower and I would be delighted if you could drop in for tea at the White House. Looking at the calendar, I suggest Monday evening, March ninth, say at five o'clock.

With best wishes and respectful regards.

Sincerely,

Dwight D. Eisenhower

A majority of the large teas given at the White House were preceded by a tour. Shown here is an admittance card to the White House through the East Entrance that was used for a gathering of this type.

Above: Invitation from the White House
Courtesy of Beulah Munshower Sommer

When Mrs. Eisenhower entertained at tea, from time to time the President requested that the names of those who came be recorded—he wanted to come over and greet the guests. The President received the members of the Supreme Court in his study for tea at 5:30 P.M. in February 1955. Present were Honorable Earl Warren, Chief Justice Hon. Hugo L. Black, Hon. Stanley Reed, Hon. Felix Frankfurter, Hon. William O. Douglas, Hon. Harold H. Burton, Hon. Tom C. Clark, Hon. Sherman Minton, Hon. Herbert Brownell, Jr., the Attorney General, Hon. Simon E. Sobeloff, the Solicitor General, Mr. Harold B. Willey, Clerk of the Supreme Court, Mr. T. Perry Lippitt, Marshal of the Supreme Court, and Mr. Walter Wyatt, Reporter of Decisions of the Supreme Court. One cannot help but wonder what the conversation involved!

A remarkable tea was held in April 1959. All of those present were descendants of the following presidents, from sons and daughters to great, great, great, great, great, great grandchildren: George Washington, John Adams, Thomas Jefferson, James Madison, John Quincy Adams, John Tyler, Abraham Lincoln, Andrew Johnson, Ulysses Grant, Rutherford B. Hayes, James A. Garfield, Grover Cleveland, Benjamin Harrison, Theodore Roosevelt, William Howard Taft, Woodrow Wilson, Calvin Coolidge, Herbert Hoover, Franklin Delano Roosevelt, and Dwight D. Eisenhower.

In 1960 Mrs. Eisenhower gave her last afternoon tea party, for her sister's daughter's début. Five hundred guests gathered in the Green Room and two tea tables were set up for the occasion.

The President and his wife were given a number of tea sets from visiting heads of state. The Meissen set from Chancellor Adenauer of Germany included a porcelain tea caddy.

Left and above: Meissen porcelain teacups and saucers, teapot, and tea caddy, eighteenth century.

Photographs courtesy of Dwight D. Eisenhower Library/ National Park Service.

When Eisenhower was Chief of Staff after World War II, he had occasion to entertain former British Ambassador Lord Halifax and his wife at tea. . . . just as Mrs. Eisenhower was beginning to pour the tea, Eisenhower said, "Would anybody rather have a drink?" "Well . . ." said Halifax hesitantly. "No you don't!" cried Mrs. Eisenhower. "I went to all sorts of trouble to get the sort of tea Ike told me he used to have with you in England. Now you take your tea, and after that you can have a drink."

Right and above: Japanese porcelain teapot and teacup and saucer; colored glazes of rusts, blues, browns, greens, and golds. Between the colors are depicted small faces of Chinese men.

Photographs courtesy of
Dwight D. Eisenhower Library/National
Park Service.

John F. Kennedy
Jacqueline Lee Bouvier

Long before John Kennedy became President, his mother was sipping tea with Sir Thomas Lipton. When Rose Fitzgerald married Joseph P. Kennedy, they received a beautiful wedding gift of some Royal Doulton teacups used on Sir Thomas Lipton's yacht, the *Erin*.

The tea party was one of John Fitzgerald Kennedy's favorite and most effective campaign devices. Kennedy was known for his well-timed quips. At one tea party he told the women why he was so optimistic about winning the election. "In the first place, for some strange reason there are more women than men in Massachusetts, and they live longer. Secondly," he went on, "my grandfather, the late John F. Fitzgerald, ran for the United States Senate thirty-six years ago against my opponent's grandfather, Henry Cabot Lodge, and he lost by only 30,000 votes in an election where women were not allowed to vote. I hope that by impressing the female electorate I can more than take up the slack." Flanked by his sisters Patricia, Jean, Eunice, and his mother Rose, the caption reads, "In the race against incumbent Henry Cabot Lodge, Jr. for the U.S. senate in 1952, Kennedy teas proved a potent weapon in the campaign arsenal."

Opposite page, top: Rose Kennedy, her sister, and a friend, with Sir Thomas Lipton.

Opposite page, center: Royal Doulton teacups and saucers.
Photographs courtesy of National Park Service, John F. Kennedy National Historic Site.

Right: John F. Kennedy outside his Georgetown home.
Photograph courtesy of John F. Kennedy Library.

John describes when he met Jacqueline Lee Bouvier at a dinner: "I leaned over the asparagus and asked her for a date." He soon discovered the beautiful young "Jackie" was intelligent and artistic. Their wedding at Newport, Rhode Island, in 1953 attracted national publicity. With aplomb and éclat the charismatic couple won the hearts of Americans as his energetic campaign for the presidency in 1960 sent him and his young family to be the residents of the White House.

The Khruschevs, at the Vienna Summit Meeting in June 1961, gave the President and Mrs. Kennedy a handsome enamelled cloisonné Russian tea set. However, it was not actually used by the Kennedys while they were in the White House.

Right: Cloisonné Russian tea set.
Photographs courtesy of John F. Kennedy Library.

Right: Mrs. Kennedy with Mrs. Khruschev having tea, 7 June 1961.

Opposite page, bottom, left to right: John F. Kennedy with his mother Rose and sisters.
Photograph by Lenscraft of Boston.

John F. Kennedy at a tea party, 1952; and
Eunice Kennedy at a tea party in '52.
Photographs courtesy of John F. Kennedy Library.

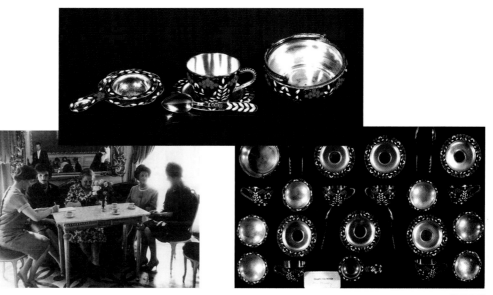

Jacqueline's great interest in art and history inspired her to devote much time bringing awareness to Americans that the White House is a museum full of history and art. She invited all Americans through the White House doors in her 1962 television tour of our First Family's home.

Among the many teas that Mrs. Kennedy hosted were: a tea for the American Society of Newspaper Editors' wives, the Special Committee for White House Paintings, the Diplomatic Reception Room donors, the American Institute of Interior Designers, and members of the National Trust for Historic Preservation. Special teas were held to honor wives of a number of ambassadors who had recently been posted to Washington, D.C. One of these teas welcomed women from Tunisia, Upper Volta, Italy, Poland, Central African Republic, Ceylon, Nepal, South Korea, Congo, and Sénégal.

Above: Jacqueline Kennedy with guests, April 1961.

Left: Jacqueline Kennedy with ambassadors' wives at a tea in September 1961.
Photographs courtesy of John F. Kennedy Library.

The Kennedy children, John and Caroline, had an English nanny, Maude Shaw. Miss Shaw remembered when they first moved to the White House: "Everyone settled down easily in the house, and every afternoon Mrs. Kennedy came upstairs to play with the baby. They were very pleasant afternoons; with the sun streaming in on us, we chatted about the child's progress and nibbled *petit beurre* biscuits with our English-style afternoon tea.... ...No words can ever really tell how closely bound I felt toward these children and their parents. For over seven years I was part of them and they will always be part of me." No doubt the children had tea with their nanny regularly. It is well known that Mrs. Kennedy guarded her children's privacy, although a photographer captured a precious moment of Caroline and John at a tea party on the White House lawn.

We saw John and Jackie's family grow up, even after President Kennedy's assassination. The Kennedy White House years are part of our national history, frozen in time. Many of us continued to view from our living rooms the triumphs and tragedies of their lives on our national stage through television and the press. While visiting England in 1965, Jacqueline, Caroline, and John had tea with Her Majesty Queen Elizabeth II at Windsor Castle.

As John F. Kennedy, Jr. emerged out of the shadow of earlier tragedy, his full measure of adventure marked the end of a century of the Fitzgerald and Kennedy family's presence, sadly punctuated by his untimely death with his wife, Carolyn, and her sister Lauren in a plane crash in July, 1999. Our nation mourned as the smiling and playful little boy America adopted as their "son" disappeared into legend along with his father.

During the 1960 presidential campaign Mrs. Johnson attended a series of teas in Texas. As First Lady, her social entertainment office lists so many teas that only a sample is mentioned here: National Council of Jewish Women, Internal Revenue Service wives, Committee for the Preservation of the White House, International Congress of Archivists, and Girl Guides and Girl Scouts.

A few weeks before the Johnson moved into the White House, Mrs. John F. Kennedy invited Mrs. Lyndon Johnson for tea to discuss the housekeeping details. She wrote in *A White House Diary*: "A lovely tea table was spread, and we sat down together in the private sitting room—the family sitting room on the second floor called the West Hall." When the Johnsons moved into the White House in December of 1963, Mrs. Johnson told her Press Secretary Liz Carpenter to be sure that the fire was lighted in the library for briefings and to have hot tea ready.

Her diary mentions having had tea with Alice Roosevelt Longworth several times; once Alice brought along her grandchild to tea. Mrs. Johnson knew that Lyndon liked Mrs. Longworth because he recognized that they shared the same strong, untamed spirit. When James Egan from Good Housekeeping interviewed Mrs. Johnson about her future plans in September 1968, they drank spiced tea together in the Lincoln Sitting Room. The First Lady speaks of an amusing incident when she walked into her husband's bedroom and found Richard Nixon sitting talking to Lyndon, who was stretched out in his pajamas, drinking tea.

"Lady Bird" always seemed to have a cup of tea at hand. She was fortified by tea with the many duties of First Lady, wife, and mother. Her daughters shared her fondness for tea. Luci and Pat received an exquisite silver tea service as a wedding gift from the Diplomatic Corps, and Lynda had tea with H.R.H. Princess Benedikte of Denmark.

Like her predecessor Mamie Eisenhower, Lady Bird Johnson invited families of previous presidents to tea. On March 2, 1967, her diary states: "Today I welcomed as houseguests members of the intimate family circles of former Presidents—Charles Taft, whose father, William Howard Taft, became President in 1909; Mrs. van Seagraves, FDR's granddaughter ("Sistie" Dahl), who lived here a while with her mother, Anna Roosevelt, and visited often during the thirteen Roosevelt years; Barbara Eisenhower, so fresh, wholesome, and pretty; and Margaret Truman, who arrived late because she had taken the train—she doesn't like airplanes. Her quietly sophisticated husband, Clifton Daniel, had arrived before.

We all sat around in the West Hall with a cup of tea and talked about their life and times here—..."

Lyndon Johnson, while he was President, drank only tea or Fresca®. Lady Bird Johnson remarked in her diary, and we agree, "How many things are launched under the name of a tea!"

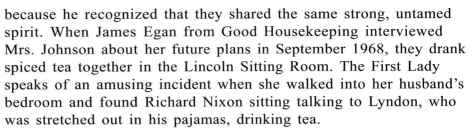

There are numerous references to tea in the files of the Nixon Administration. Pat Nixon took a gift of tea to Raisa Gorbachev.

We are indeed fortunate to have a photograph of Mrs. Nixon with the president of the Welcome to Washington International Club, Natalie J. Whitney, at a White House tea in April, 1969.

President and Mrs. Nixon were given several tea sets as gifts. One is a Sèvres cobalt blue and gold porcelain with an RMN monogram. It was presented to President Nixon by Charles de Gaulle in 1960. It consists of a teapot, sugar bowl, creamer, and eleven cups and saucers.

Below: Sèvres cobalt blue and gold porcelain tea set, with an RMN monogram.
Photograph courtesy of The Richard Nixon Library & Birthplace.

There is a Russian tea set which was a head of state gift to the Nixons during their visit to Moscow in 1972. They also received a small Chinese Yixing teapot that was a gift to President Nixon on one of his post-presidential visits to China. While in China, the Nixons bought their daughter Julie Nixon Eisenhower a Chinese tea set.

Even the President was given detailed information and instructions in 1970, regarding his appearance at a tea that Mrs. Nixon planned and hosted for White House volunteers.

Above: Mrs. Nixon with members of the Welcome to Washington International Club and their president Natalie J. Whitney.
Photograph courtesy of Natalie J. Whitney

Right: Chinese Yixing teapot.
Photograph courtesy of The Richard Nixon Library & Birthplace.

President and Mrs. Ford often entertained extensively at tea. Even in their private quarters, President Ford would often make his own breakfast, consisting of grapefruit, English muffins, and tea.

Mrs. Ford, a courageous and candid First Lady, promoted open discussion on a previously almost taboo subject, breast cancer, when she underwent successful surgery in 1974.

A former Martha Graham dancer and John Robert Powers fashion model, Betty Ford serenely accepted her unexpected role as First Lady, deeming it a challenge.

As the President's wife, it was customary for Mrs. Ford to have tea with wives of visiting heads of state. One of her teas was given in the White House

Below: President Gerald Ford
Photograph courtesy UPI/CORBIS-BETTMANN.

residence for Mrs. Valéry Giscard d'Estaing. Present at the time was Mrs. Jacques Kosciusko-Morizet, wife of the ambassador from France to the United States, and Mrs. Steward W. Rockwell, wife of the Deputy Chief of Protocol. President Ford dropped in to join the ladies that day.

While in the White House, the Fords received several silver tea sets from the heads of state of Egypt, Indonesia, Romania, and Republic of the Sudan.

Below: Mrs. Ford entertaining Mrs. Valéry Giscard d'Estaing for tea in the White House residence.

Photograph courtesy of Gerald R. Ford Library, Ann Arbor, Michigan.

James Earl Carter, Jr.
Rosalynn Smith

Jimmy Carter graduated from the U. S. Naval Academy, served in the navy until his father died and then came home to run the family business. He married Rosalynn Smith, who became his partner both in politics and business. He entered politics and served in the Georgia state senate, as governor, and then became the President of the United States, succeeding President Ford. Although the Carters were inclined to be less glamorous in their social obligations, they did entertain a great deal.

Mrs. Carter was inundated with invitations to host teas. She was able to accommodate most of the requests that are part of the heavy White House social schedule. Taking a strong interest in the arts, she regularly invited musicians to perform at White House teas and other events.

During the many talks between Menachem Begin and Anwar Sadat, Mrs. Carter entertained at tea for both Mrs. Begin and Mrs. Sadat.

When the cherry trees were in full blossom, President Carter entertained Mr. Sadat at tea in the White House garden. Inside the White House, Mrs. Sadat was the guest of honor at a tea party where the First

Above: President Jimmy Carter and President Anwar Sadat.

Below: Rosalynn Carter with Mrs. Anwar Sadat and Mrs. Mondale.

Above: Rosalynn Carter with
Mrs. Menachem Begin.

Below: Prime Minister Kriangsak Choman
and Mrs. Choman present a celadon tea set
to President and Mrs. Carter. Teapot
pictured above.

Lady and Mrs. Mondale sat on either side
of her at individual tea tables.

At a tea honoring Mrs. Begin, iced tea, a
favorite with the southern Carters, was
served.

A handsome celadon teapot was a gift
from the Kingdom of Thailand. It was
presented to President and Mrs. Carter on
the occasion of a state visit by Prime
Minister Kriangsak Choman and
Khunying (Mrs.) Virat Chomanan in 1979.

Below: Rosalynn Carter taking time
to chat with U.S. Marine harpist.

All photographs courtesy of
Jimmy Carter Library, Atlanta, GA.

Fortieth President

Ronald Wilson Reagan
Nancy Davis

Facing page top: Nancy Reagan having tea with Princess Benedikte of Denmark in the Yellow Room at the White House.

Facing Page center: Nancy Reagan having tea with Queen Noor of Jordan in the Red Room at the White House.

Facing page bottom left: Nancy Reagan having tea with Mrs. Nakasone of Japan in the Green Room at the White House.

Below: HRH Prince Charles and HRH Princess Diana with President and Mrs. Reagan at the White House.

Photographs courtesy of Ronald Reagan Library.

Ronald Reagan and Nancy Davis met in California while he was president of the Screen Actors Guild. They married in 1952 and played opposite each other in her last film, *Hellcats of the Navy*, in 1956. She adapted well to her new role as a governor's wife when he won the election in California in 1967.

After they took up residence in the White House, along with the usual state social functions, Nancy hosted many intimate teas in the Red Room, Green Room, and Yellow Room; the President frequently joined her. Prince Charles and Princess Diana came to have tea with the Reagans in the Yellow Room.

In contrast to the simpler style of the Carter administration, the President and Mrs. Reagan entertained lavishly.

A British pottery made caricature teapots, sugars, and creamers of Margaret Thatcher, Prince Charles, Princess Diana, Ronald Reagan, and other world figures.

Below: Ronald Reagan teapot towering above the White House and the United States Flag novelty teapots.
Photograph by Pearl Dexter.

All evidence points to George Bush as being a tea drinker. It was a well-known fact that President Bush liked green tea. In an interview in October 1997, the chef from Camp David, Maryland, Willie Nocon, confirmed this preference. A letter received from Mrs. Bush's staff assistant states, "Mrs. Bush loves to drink tea. In fact, while in China Mrs. Bush drank green tea all of the time. ..." The President and his First Lady had a tea reception for Hanzhi Zhang, the widow of the former Chinese minister when she came to Washington.

The First Lady's scheduling office planned and coordinated White House teas; refreshments were arranged through the White House Chief Usher. While President Bush was in office, Mrs. Bush regularly hosted afternoon teas in the residence and on the state floors of the White House. These gatherings were attended by a wide variety of groups and individuals. Guests often included friends, White House staff, members of public service organizations, and spouses of visiting foreign dignitaries.

Mrs. Bush requests the pleasure of your company at a tea to be held at The White House with Members of The International Clubs and International Neighbors Clubs on Monday afternoon, April 30, 1990 at two-thirty o'clock

Above: Barbara Bush entertaining HRH Princess Margaret of the Netherlands.

Facing page top: President Bush with Hanzhi Zhang, widow of former Chinese Foreign Minister Qiao Guanhua.

Facing page center: Mrs. Bush with Mrs. Turgut Azal of Turkey.

Facing page bottom: Mrs. Bush with Mrs. Aristides Peieura of Cape Verde.

Below: President Bush and President Boris Yeltsin in Moscow at a farewell tea.

Mrs. Turgut Azal of Turkey and Mrs. Aristides Peieura of Cape Verde joined the First Lady for tea on separate occasions. It is amusing to note that Millie, the First Dog, was included at a tea party attended by Princess Margaret of the Netherlands.

President Bush visited Russia in 1993, and on one occasion he attended a farewell tea with President Yeltsin in Moscow. He was presented with a Gzhel pottery tea set decorated with an old pattern—the milk pitcher is shaped like a whimsical fish.

Tea is a major international beverage, evidenced by the many tea sets that presidents have received. Romania and Germany each gave President and Mrs. Bush a fine example of their country's porcelain.

Below: "Gzhel" pottery tea set given to President and Mrs. Bush during their visit to Moscow on January 3, 1993.

All photographs courtesy of George Bush Presidential Library.

Tea has certainly played a role in the lives of Bill and Hillary Clinton, from the World Peace Summit in 1997 to Mrs. Clinton's visits to Northern Ireland and Russia.

During the preparations for the World Peace Summit in Denver, The Fort, a well-known Denver area restaurant, contacted Harney and Sons Fine Teas. They were asked to create a special blend for a reception in honor of the eight heads of state who were expected to attend the summit. They were: President Jacques Chirac of France, Chancellor Helmut Kohl of Germany, Prime Minister Tony Blair of the United Kingdom, Prime Minister Jean Chrétien of Canada, Prime Minister Ryutaro Hashimoto of Japan, Prime Minister Romano Prodi of Italy, President Boris Yeltsin of Russia, and President Bill Clinton.

John Harney decided to include eight teas from eight different tea regions: Keemun, Yunnan, Panyang Congou, Assam, Ceylon, Kenya, Darjeeling, and Ceylon Silver Tips. These are all excellent black teas, topped with silver tips for their visual and taste quality. The blending of eight teas to create one, extraordinary new tea would symbolize the gathering of eight world leaders to promote world peace.

President Bill Clinton and Prime Minister Tony Blair sipped tea at the White House from special china mugs embellished with gold eagles that had been ordered from Lenox.

A recent Russian edition of *Good Housekeeping* magazine (known in Russian as *Home's Hearth*) featured Hillary Rodham Clinton with Naina Yeltsin on the cover, enjoying a cup of tea. The two First Ladies held a panel discussion on issues of importance to women, emphasizing similarities in the lives of Russian and American women.

Below: Cover of Russian edition of *Good Housekeeping*, known as *Home's Hearth*.

On a visit to Belfast, Ireland, Mrs. Clinton encouraged politicians to sort out their problems by getting together over many cups of tea.

Judy and Nancy Pickney, designers and ceramists from Arkansas, presented Mrs. Clinton with a teapot, four cups, and a tray when they were invited to the White House to see how Hillary had decorated the presidential living quarters with some of their pieces.

A teapot and teacup are always included in the Clintons' Christmas card design, reflecting their fondness for tea.

Right: Autographed photograph of Hillary Rodham Clinton with Judy and Nancy Pickney at the White House.

Photograph courtesy of Judy Pickney.

To Judy and Nancy Pickney with best wishes, and thanks!
Hillary Rodham Clinton

Bibliography

Adams, John. *Diary and Autobiography*. Vols. I, II, III, IV, and *The Early Years*. L. H. Butterfield, ed. Belknap Press of Harvard, 1961.

Adams, Samuel Hopkins. *Incredible Era*. Boston: Houghton Mifflin Co., 1939.

Aikman, Lonnelle. *The Living White House*. Washington, DC: The White House Historical Association, 1996.

Alexander, Holmes Moss. *The American Talleyrand*. New York: Harper, 1935.

Ammon, Henry. *James Monroe*. New York: McGraw Hill, 1971.

Anthony, Carl Sferrazza. *First Ladies*. New York: William Morrow and Co., Vol. I 1990, Vol. II 1991.

Arnett, Ethel Stephens. *Mrs. James Madison, The Incomparable Dolley*. Greensboro, NC: Piedmont Press, 1972.

Baldridge, Letitia. *Of Diamonds and Diplomats*. Boston: Houghton Mifflin Co., 1968.

Bergeron, Paul H. *The Presidency of James K. Polk*. Lawrence: University of Kansas, 1987.

Bobbe, Dorothie. *Abigail Adams, The Second First Lady*. New York: Minton, Balch, and Co., 1929.

Boller, Paul. *Presidential Wives*. New York: Oxford University Press, 1988.

Burke, Pauline Wilcox. *Emily Donelson of Tennessee*. Richmond, VA: Garrett and Massie, Inc., 1942. 2 vols.

Bush Presidential Library Papers

Cannon, Poppy, and Brooks, Patricia. *The Presidents' Cookbook*. New York: Funk and Wagnalls, 1968.

Caroli, Betty Boyd. *America's First Ladies*. New York: Reader's Digest Association, Inc. 1996.

Caroli, Betty Boyd. *First Ladies*. New York: Oxford University Press, 1987.

Carson, Barbara. *Ambitious Appetites*. American Institute of Architects Press, 1990.

Carter Presidential Library Papers

Cavanah, Frances. *They Lived in the White House*. Philadelphia: Macrae Smith Co., 1959.

Claxton, Jimmie Lou Sparkman. *88 Years with Sarah Polk*. New York: Vantage Press, 1972.

Clay-Clayton, Virginia. *A Belle of the Fifties*. New York: Doubleday, Page, and Co., 1904.

Coleman, Elizabeth Tyler. *Priscilla Cooper Tyler and the American Scene*. Alabama: University of Alabama Press, 1955.

Coolidge, Grace. *An Autobiography*. Edited by Lawrence E. Wikander and Robert H. Ferrell. Worland, Wyoming: High Plains Publishing Co., 1992 (By The Calvin Coolidge Memorial Foundation, Inc.)

Crook, William Henry. *Through Five Administrations*. New York: Harper and Brothers, 1910.

DeGregorio, William A. *The Complete Book of the Presidents*. 5th ed. New York: 1997.

Detweiler, Susan Gray. *George Washington's Chinaware*. New York: Abrams, 1982

Eisenhower Presidential Library Papers

Ervin, Janet. *The White House Cookbook*. Chicago: Follett Publishing Co., 1964.

Fields, Alonzo. *My 21 Years in the White House*. New York: Coward-McCann, Inc., 1960.

First Ladies Cook Book. New York: GMP Publishers, 1982.

Fitzpatrick, John G., ed. *Writings of George Washington*, 39 volumes. Vols. 2, 3, 8, 12, 16, 23, 25, 27, 28, 29, 35, 36, 37. Washington, DC: U.S. Government Printing Office, 1931.

Ford Presidential Library Papers

Freidel, Frank. *Our Country's Presidents*. Washington, DC: National Geographic Society, 1966.

Freidel, Frank. *The Presidents of the United States of America*. Washington, DC: White House Historical Association, 1995.

Fritz, Jean. *George Washington's Breakfast*. New York: Coward-McCann, Inc., 1969.

Graf, Leroy P., and Ralph W. Haskins, editors. *The Papers of Andrew Johnson*, Vol. 3. Knoxville, TN: University of Tennessee Press, 1972.

Grant, Mrs. Ulysses S., ed. John Y. Simon. *The Personal Memoirs of Julia Dent Grant*. Carbondale: Southern Illinois University Press, 1975.

Grayson, Cary T. *Woodrow Wilson, An Intimate Memoir*. Washington, DC: Potomac Books, Inc. Publishers, 1977.

Greer, Emily. *First Lady, the Life of Lucy Webb Hayes*. Kent State University Press, 1984.

Helms, Edith. *The Captains and The Kings*. New York: G. P. Putnam's Sons, 1954.

Hilowitz, Beverley, and Green, Susan Eikov, eds. *Great Historic Places*. New York: Simon and Schuster, 1980.

Hoover, Irwin Hood. *Forty-Two Years in the White House*. Boston: Houghton Mifflin Co., 1934.

Hoover Presidential Library Papers

Jaffray, Elizabeth. *Secrets of the White House*. New York: Cosmopolitan Book Co., 1927.

Jefferson Papers from Monticello, Virginia

Jeffries, Ora Griffin. *In and Out of the White House*. New York: Wilfred Funk, 1960.

Jennings, John. *Clipper Ship Days*. New York: Random House, 1952.

Jensen, Amy LaFollette. *The White House and Its Thirty-Five Families*. New York: McGraw Hill, 1971.

Johnson, Lady Bird. *A White House Diary*. New York: Holt, Rinehart, and Winston, 1970.

Johnson, Lyndon B. Presidential Library Papers

Kennedy Presidential Library Papers

Ketcham, Ralph. *James Madison*. Charlottesville, VA: University Press of Virginia, 1990.

Klapthor, Margaret Brown. *Official White House China*. Washington, DC: Smithsonian Institution Press, 19

Klapthor, Margaret Brown. *The First Ladies*. Washington, DC: White House Historical Association in cooperation with the National Geographic Society, 1995.

Langston-Harrison, Lee. *A Presidential Legacy*. Fredericksburg, VA: The James Monroe Museum, 1997.

Leech, Margaret. *In the Days of McKinley*. New York: Harper and Brothers, 1959.

Leish, Kenneth W. *The White House, A History of the Presidents*. New York: Newsweek, 1977.

Lewis, Ethel. *The White House*. Dodd, Mead, and Co., 1937.

Lincoln, Letter from Springfield, Ohio

Lincoln, Anne H. *The Kennedy White House Parties*. New York: Viking Press, 1967.

Morgan, George. *The Life of James Monroe*. Boston: Small, Maynard and Co., 1921.

Morris, Sylvia Jukes. *Edith Kermit Roosevelt. Portrait of a First Lady*. New York: Geoghegan, Inc., 198(

Nesbitt, Henrietta. *White House Diary*. New York: Doubleday, 1948.

Nixon Presidential Library Papers

Nixon Papers, Archives II, Adelphi, Maryland

Ohio Historical Society, Harding Papers

Peterson, Norma Lois. *The Presidencies of William Henry Harrison and John Tyler*. Lawrence, Kansas: Univ Press of Kansas, 1989.

Pitch, Anthony S. *Presidential Trivia*. Potomac, Maryland: Mino Publications, 1993.

Rayback, Robert J. *Millard Fillmore*. Buffalo,NY: Henry Stewart Inc., 1959.

Reagan Presidential Library Papers

Reeves, Thomas C. *Gentleman Boss*. New York: Knopf, 1975.

Roosevelt, Eleanor. *Book of Common Sense Etiquette*. New York: Macmillan Co., 1962.

Roosevelt, Eleanor. *My Days*. New York: Dodge Publishing Co., 1938.

Roosevelt, Eleanor. *This I Remember*. New York: Harper and Brothers, 1949.

Roosevelt, Franklin D. Presidential Library Papers

Ross, Ishbel. *Grace Coolidge and Her Era*. New York: Dodd, Mead, and Co., 1962.

Ross, Ishbel. *Proud Kate*. New York: Harper, 1953.

Ross, Ishbel. *The General's Wife, The Life of Mrs. Ulysses S. Grant*. New York: Dodd, Mead, and Co., 1959.

Rysavy, Francis. *A Treasury of White House Cooking*. New York: Putnam, 1972.

Rysavy, Francis. *White House Chef*. New York: C. P. Putnam's Sons, 1957.

Seager, Robert II. *And Tyler Too*. New York: McGraw Hill Book Co., Inc., 1963.

Seale, William. *The President's House*. Vols. I and II. Washington, DC: White House Historical Association with cooperation of the National Geographic Society, 1986.

Shaw, Maud. *White House Nannie*. New York: New York Library, 1966.

Sievers, Harry J. *Benjamin Harrison*. Vol. 3. New York: Bobbs-Merrill Co. Inc., 1968.

Spielman, William Carl. *William McKinley*. New York: Exposition Press, 1954.

Spillman, Jane Shadel. *White House Glassware*. White House Historical Association with cooperation of the National Geographic Society and Corning Museum of Glass, 1989.

Smith, Maria. *Entertaining in the White House*. Washington, DC: Acropolis Books, 1967.

Steinberg, Alfred. *Mrs. Roosevelt*. New York: Putnam, 1958.

Taft, Mrs. William Howard. *Recollections of Full Years*. New York: Dodd, Mead, and Co., 1914.

Thayer, Henry. *Jacqueline Kennedy, The White House Years*. Boston: Little, Brown, 1971.

Truman Presidential Library Papers

Tyler, Lyon G. *The Letters and Times of the Tylers*, Volume II. New York: DaCapo Press, 1970.

Tugwell, Rexford G. *Grover Cleveland*. New York: Macmillan, 1968.

Washington Papers from Mount Vernon, Virginia

West, J. B. *Upstairs at the White House*. New York: Coward, McCann, and Geoghegan, Inc., 1973.

Wilson, Edith Bolling. *My Memoir*. New York: The Bobbs-Merrill Co., 1939.

World Book of America's Presidents. Chicago: World Book, Inc., 1988.

Winston, Robert Watsons. *Andrew Johnson*. New York: H. Holt and Co., 1928.

Wooten, James E. *Elizabeth Kortright Monroe*. College of William and Mary, 1990.

The White House: Resources for Research at the Library of Congress. Washington, DC: the Library of Congress, 1992.